Happiness is planning a trip to somewhere new with someone you love.

Introduction

Welcome, fellow adventurers! Your weekend getaways are about to get one hell of an upgrade...

Whether you're planning a surprise trip for your significant other or simply looking to escape the hustle and bustle of everyday life, this guide has got your back.

We understand that planning a weekend getaway can be stressful and time consuming, which is why we've compiled this unique and exciting guidebook. Each UK destination contains must-see locations, practical tips and stress saving hacks to make your trip planning a breeze.

So, grab your other half and get ready for a weekend filled with love, laughter, and unforgettable memories. This guide will not only help you plan the perfect getaway, but it will also leave you wanting more. Get ready to fall in love all over again on your next couples weekend away...

What's all the fuss about?

Well actually, there is no fuss!

We'd like to introduce you to the future of guide-books! We've taken a new and refreshing approach to travel guides. What sets us apart is our unique writing style. Imagine having a casual conversation with a friend over a few pints, that's the tone we use in our guides. We want you to feel like you are getting advice from a fellow traveller, making it easy to understand and completely relatable.

Our guides are not just based on research, but also on personal experiences. We have a team of experienced travellers who have visited destinations across the UK and have first hand knowledge to share with you. This ensures that our recommendations are authentic and unbiased.

Now that we're done with the introductions, let's get planning your next unforgettable weekend away...

How to use this book?

1. Start by choosing your desired UK location from the guidebook. This could be a city, town, or countryside destination. Take a look at the rating scale to get an idea of each location. This can help you prioritise which places to visit first.

2. Once you have selected your location, check the travel times provided for each location. This will help you plan your trip and determine the best mode of transportation to reach your destination.

3. Check the *'best time to visit'* section for your chosen location. This will give you an idea of when the weather is most pleasant, when popular events or festivals take place, and when the destination is least crowded.

4. Explore the *'best places to eat and drink'* section for recommendations on local cuisine and popular restaurants and bars in the area. Vegan options are indicated by the leaf icon.

5. Check the accommodation section for suggested hotel and B&B options across all budgets.

6. Use the suggested itinerary as a guide to help you plan your trip, but don't be afraid to deviate and add your own unique experiences. Our itineraries presume you'll arrive Friday morning, but don't sweat it if you can't arrive until the evening.

7. Delve into the *'must see locations'* section. We've handpicked a selection of attractions and landmarks in the area that you shouldn't miss. We've split these into sections, so whether you're looking for a weekend of relaxation, you're seeking adventure or if you have a budget to stick to - there are locations and attractions to cover all eventualities. We recommend using Google Maps on your smartphone to navigate each destination.

8. As you explore your chosen location, keep the guidebook handy for reference and don't forget to complete the travel journal, it'll be great to look back on in years to come.

9. Remember to have fun and embrace the sense of adventure by going off the beaten track and exploring beyond the recommendations in the guidebook.

Scotland

Loch Lomond

Best For: Outdoor adventure, epic scenery, walking & boat rides.

City breaks not your cup of tea? Take a trip to Loch Lomond to experience some of the finest landscapes Scotland has to offer. The National Park encompasses around 720 square miles and can be explored on foot, on a bike, or even by boat on the water itself. If you like an active holiday that you can take at your own pace, this one could be for you. We highly recommend kayaking on the loch, it's an experience you won't forget in a hurry!

Loch Cruises

Romance ♥♥♥♥♡
Food & Drink ♥♥♥♡♡
Things To See ♥♥♥♥♡
Natural Beauty ♥♥♥♥♥

Kayaking on Loch Lomond

Drive Time to Loch Lomond
From London | 8 hours
From Manchester | 4 hours
From Newcastle | 3 hours
From Birmingham | 5 hours
From Cardiff | 7 hours

Train Duration to Loch Lomond
From London | 11.5 hours
From Manchester | 7 hours
From Newcastle | 6 hours
From Birmingham | 11 hours
From Cardiff | 13 hours

Best Time to Visit...
Summer - Some attractions close in the colder months and re-open again in the Spring, so make sure you time your visit right depending on what you want to do and see.
Autumn - If you'd prefer a quieter trip, we'd recommend visiting in the autumn or winter.

Best Places to Eat & Drink...

Skoosh | Cheap and cheerful breakfasts
50 Main Street, Drymen, LL & The Trossachs National Park G63 0BG

Coach House Coffee Shop | Coffee & cake in a cosy setting
Church Road, Luss, LL & The Trossachs National Park G83 8NN

The Pier Café | Lunch spot with a stunning view
Loch Katrine, Stronachlachar, LL & The Trossachs National Park FK8 3TY

The Clachan Inn | Scotland's oldest licensed pub
2 The Square Drymen Sq, Drymen, LL & The Trossachs National Park G63 0BL

The Slanj Loch Lomond | Family-run restaurant
Station Road, Tarbet, LL & The Trossachs National Park G83 7DA

Top Tip: Look out for an array of wildlife across the Loch Lomond
& The Trossachs National Park, such as Highland Cattle, Roe Deer,
Red Deer and Red Squirrels (to name a few).

Loch Lomond

Accommodation

£

Oak Tree Inn | 0136 087 0357
Balmaha Road, Balmaha G63 0JQ

Lomond Woods Holiday Park Lodges | 0125 087 8123
Tullichewan Old Luss Road, Balloch G83 8QP

Gowanlea Guest House | 0138 975 2456
Drymen Road, Balloch G83 8HS

££

The Inn on Loch Lomond | 0143 686 0430
Luss G83 8PD

The Loch Lomond Arms Hotel | 0143 686 0420
Main Road, Luss G83 8NY

Culag Lochside Self Catering | 0791 813 7021
Argyll & Stirling, Luss G83 8PD

£££

Waterfront Luxury Lodges | 0136 087 0144
Main Road, Balmaha G63 0JQ

Lodge on Loch Lomond | 0143 686 0201
Route A82, Luss G83 8PA

Cameron House on Loch Lomond | 0138 931 2210
Loch Lomond G83 8QZ

A Weekend Itinerary...

Day	Morning	Afternoon	Evening
Friday	Arrive in Loch Lomond	Cruise on the Loch	Dinner at Loch Lomond Shores
Saturday	Try Loch Lomond pony trekking	Visit the Loch Lomond Bird of Prey Centre	Enjoy some pub-grub at The Clachan Inn
Sunday	Walk along the West Highland Way	Enjoy kayaking on Loch Lomond	Travel home

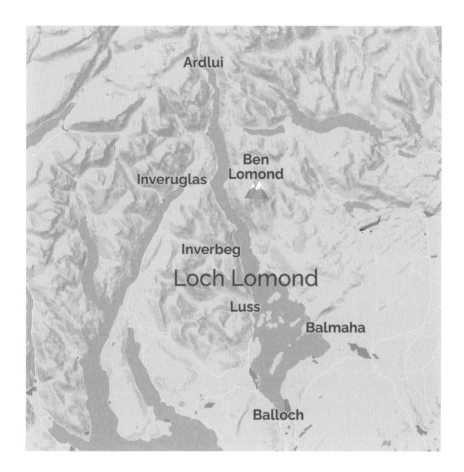

Best way to explore Loch Lomond...

Using a vehicle to get around Loch Lomond is an obvious choice; however, there's lots of other ways to explore. Catch a bus from one village to another or travel across the loch by boat. Hiring a bike can also be one of the best ways to discover this mighty and magnificent area. Some hire companies offer collection and drop off at different locations, an option certainly worth considering.

 Did you know?

Loch Lomond is home to 22 islands and 27 islets (very small islands). Three of which are in the care of conservation agencies, the rest of the islands are privately owned.

Top picks for slowing down...

Loch Cruises
Various Departure Points

Experience some of the best views of Loch Lomond and the surrounding areas on the water. Cruise Loch Lomond over various different tours costing under £20 a ticket, including winter cruises and hop on, hop off trips. We'd recommend visiting their website for departure times and tickets ahead of your trip.

Loch Lomond Shores
Ben Lomond Way, Balloch
G83 8QL

If you're looking to indulge in some retail therapy, Loch Lomond Shores could be the perfect place to do so. Located in Balloch on the banks of the loch, there's a small collection of shops, including places to buy your Scottish souvenirs, and several restaurants and cafés to have a drink in afterwards.

Unique things to see & do...

Loch Lomond Bird of Prey Centre
Ben Lomond Way, Loch Lomond Shores, Balloch
G83 8QL

Over 40 birds of Prey and Owls reside here! Venture into the woods to watch one of the daily flying shows and learn more about the birds at the centre. If you want to get up close and personal with the centre's residents, book one of the private experiences offered all-year round.

Loch Lomond Pony Trekking
Tullichewan Farm, Upper Stoneymollan Road, Balloch
G83 8QY

Experience the beauty of Loch Lomond from a completely unique perspective. Experienced ride leaders will take you on a leisurely trek through the Scottish countryside and high into the moorland to look down onto the banks of the loch. They cater for people of all abilities, so don't worry if you haven't ridden a horse before!

Sea Life Loch Lomond
Balloch, G83 8QL

Discover Scotland's largest collection of sharks plus over 1,500 creatures (*including resident otters; Lily, Pickle & Cub*), as you explore the tropical ocean tunnel and 7 themed zones at Sea Life Loch Lomond. You could even book a '*feed the sharks*' experience. Pre-booking is essential.

Loch Lomond

Balloch Castle Country Park

Top picks for adventure seekers...

TreeZone Loch Lomond
1 Ben Lomond Way, Loch Lomond Shores, Balloch G83 8QL

Go high into the tree tops for an action-packed afternoon at TreeZone in Balloch. There's two different courses to choose from with the highest point sitting at 14 metres. TreeZone is quite pricey, costing around £24 a ticket, but if you're both adrenaline junkies who enjoy this sort of activity it's totally worth it.

Kayaking on Loch Lomond
Loch Lomond Leisure, Luss Beach G83 8PA

You've experienced Loch Lomond from the shore, so now it's time to see it from the water! Hire a single or twin kayak from Loch Lomond Leisure and explore the loch at your own pace. If you want to learn more about the area, book onto one of the company's two hour guided kayak tours.

Budget-friendly finds...

Balloch Castle Country Park
Balloch Castle Drymen Road, Balloch G83 8LX

Loch Lomond's only country park spanning 200 acres. Its castle is now derelict; however, the park still makes for a lovely stroll. Why not take a picnic if the weather is warm and enjoy loch views by the shore. Be aware that the park gets particularly busy in the summer months so parking can sometimes be tricky!

West Highland Way
Various routes across the area

The West Highland Way stretches 96 miles from Milngavie to Fort William and is a popular walking route. The route covers beautiful scenery including Mugdock Country Park, Ben Lomond, Glencoe and Glen Nevis. We'd recommend visiting the West Highland Way website to pick out the best route for you.

Our visit to Loch Lomond...

We visited...

☐ Loch Cruises   ☐ Loch Lomond Shores

☐ Loch Lomond Pony Trekking   ☐ Loch Lomond Bird of Prey Centre

☐ Sea Life Loch Lomond   ☐ TreeZone Loch Lomond

☐ Kayaking on Loch Lomond   ☐ Balloch Castle Country Park

☐ West Highland Way   ☐ ....

☐ ....   ☐ ....

☐ ....   ☐ ....

Notes...

....

....

....

....

....

....

Rating: ♡ ♡ ♡ ♡ ♡

*Our favourite photo
from the weekend*

Date:

Location:

Caption:

Edinburgh

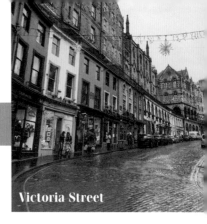

Best For: Historic sights, culture, amazing bars & Harry Potter!

The Scottish capital; historic sights, scenic views, fantastic bars and world-famous festivals. Whether you're looking for a relaxing romantic weekend or a fun-filled one with lots of activities, Edinburgh is a diverse city with something for everyone. Despite being the capital, Edinburgh is a fairly small city, and a lot of the major attractions are close together making this a great location for a short break. JK Rowling wrote Harry Potter whilst living here – so you can find magical traces of Harry Potter throughout the city too.

Victoria Street

Romance ♥♥♥♥♡
Food & Drink ♥♥♥♥♥
Things To See ♥♥♥♥♥
Natural Beauty ♥♥♥♡♡

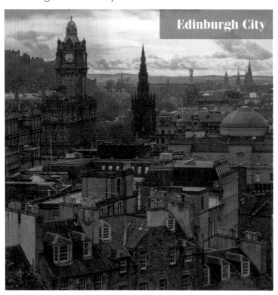

Edinburgh City

Drive Time to Edinburgh
From London | 7.5 hours
From Manchester | 4 hours
From Newcastle | 2.5 hours
From Birmingham | 6 hours
From Cardiff | 7.5 hours

Train Duration to Edinburgh
From London | 5.5 hours
From Manchester | 3.5 hours
From Newcastle | 1.5 hours
From Birmingham | 4.5 hours
From Cardiff | 6.5 hours

Best Time to Visit...
Expect the unexpected and dress accordingly!
Spring - less crowded and better chances of good weather.
August - festival month! Edinburgh International Festival, Edinburgh Fringe and Edinburgh Military Tattoo all take place in August. A great month to visit if you're attending a festival but best to avoid if not - as it will be crowded.
Winter - Incredible Christmas markets.

Best Places to Eat & Drink...

Makars Gourmet Mash Bar | Independent Scottish comfort food
9-12 Bank St, Edinburgh EH1 2LN

3 Blind Mice | Outstanding pizza restaurant & cocktail bar
19-21 Blackfriars St, Edinburgh EH1 1NB

L'escargot Bleu | French bistro serving Scottish produce
56 Broughton St, Edinburgh EH1 3SA

Lucky Yu | Japanese inspired food & amazing cocktails
53-55 Broughton Street, Edinburgh EH1 3RJ

Timberyard | Industrial-chic restaurant serving Michelin menu
10 Lady Lawson St, Edinburgh EH3 9DS

Top Tip: Head to *edinburgh.org/planning/offers-deals/* ahead of your trip to see what discounts and deals are available across attractions, eateries and transport.

Edinburgh Castle

Accommodation

£

Moxy Edinburgh Fountainbridge | 0131 378 2013
2 Freer Gait, Edinburgh EH3 9FR

Haystack Hostel (private rooms available) | 0131 557 0036
5, 3 W Register St, Edinburgh EH2 2AA

Aparthotel Adagio Edinburgh | 0131 322 8299
231 Canongate, Edinburgh EH8 8BJ

££

The Haymarket Hotel | 0131 337 1775
1 Coates Gardens, Edinburgh EH12 5LG

Old Waverley Hotel | 0131 556 4648
43 Princes St, Edinburgh EH2 2BY

Fraser Suites Edinburgh | 0131 221 7200
12, 24 St Giles' St, Edinburgh EH1 1PT

£££

Radisson Blu Hotel Edinburgh | 0131 557 9797
The Royal Mile, 80 High St, Edinburgh EH1 1TH

Cheval The Edinburgh Grand | 0131 230 0570
42 St Andrew Square, Edinburgh EH2 2AD

Hilton Edinburgh Carlton | 0131 472 3000
19 North Bridge, Edinburgh EH1 1SD

A Weekend Itinerary...

Day	Morning	Afternoon	Evening
Friday	Arrive in Edinburgh	Wander along the Royal Mile & Mary King's Close	Spend a romantic evening at the Dominion Cinema
Saturday	Visit Edinburgh Castle	Take a tour at the Scotch Whiskey Experience	Enjoy a romantic meal at Timberyard
Sunday	Hike to Arthur's Seat or enjoy afternoon tea on the Red Bus Bistro	Explore the Camera Obscura & World of Illusions	Travel home

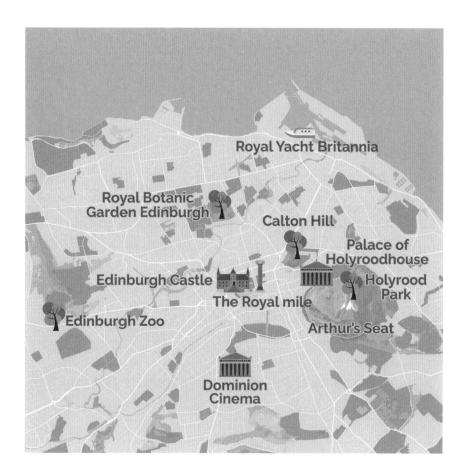

Best way to explore Edinburgh...

Despite being the capital city of Scotland, Edinburgh is relatively small and most of its major attractions are conveniently located close together, so exploring on foot is the best option. If you wanted to visit places outside the old city, the hop-on hop-off bus is a fantastic option or more physically active couples may look at renting a bike.

 Did you know?

The world's only knighted penguin lives at Edinburgh Zoo. His name is Sir Nils and he resides with the rest of the colony in Penguins Rock. His role includes inspecting the Norwegian Guard on their visits to the Scottish capital.

Top picks for slowing down...

Red Bus Bistro
Bus Stop outside the Malmaison Hotel, St Andrew Square, EH2 2AD

A different way to wind down, get a bird's eye view of Edinburgh from the top of an iconic red bus. You'll travel past a lot of Edinburgh's landmarks during the 1.5 hour experience, whilst you enjoy an afternoon tea consisting of sweet & savoury treats, a glass of fizz and tea or coffee.

Dominion Cinema
Newbattle Terrace, EH10 4RT

A luxury cinema with a romantic twist. Located in the Morningside neighbourhood, the Dominion is an old school cinema with cosy sofas, privacy screens and evening table service. Showing a great mix of new films and old classics, this is the perfect way to spend a romantic evening in Edinburgh.

Unique things to see & do...

The Scotch Whisky Experience
354 Castlehill, EH1 2NE

A complete must do for budding Scotch lovers, the immersive tours at the Scotch Whisky Experience have a few fun tricks to help fully immerse guests. If you're keen to sample some authentic Scotch Whisky then there are several tour options (the exceptional reviews may also twist your arm).

Edinburgh Castle
Castlehill, EH1 2NG

One of the city's most popular tourist attractions! Located in the heart of Edinburgh, it's one of Europe's oldest fortified places which has been dominating the city skyline since the 11th century. Its best to book tickets online as they often sell out. Visits are self-guided or you can book onto a guided tour.

The Royal Mile

Red Bus Bistro

Arthur's Seat

Top picks for adventure seekers...

Hike to Arthur's Seat
EH15 3PY

Enjoy a picturesque stroll up the remnants of an extinct volcano towering 250m above the city. From the top you'll spot some of Edinburgh's most iconic landmarks including Holyrood House, the Scottish Parliament and Edinburgh Castle. A perfect and awfully romantic place to watch the sunset.

The Real Mary King's Close
2 Warriston's Cl, EH1 1PG

Explore one of Edinburgh's most unique attractions as you delve into the darker side of the city's history. This immersive tour runs beneath the streets of The Royal Mile in a warren of alleys and abandoned houses that date back to the 17th century. We have a feeling you'll both thoroughly enjoy this highly engaging experience.

Camera Obscura & World of Illusions
549 Castlehill, EH1 2ND

Camera Obscura has over 100 illusions set across 5 floors (*please be aware there isn't a lift*) which makes for an ideal rain-day activity - a likely event in Edinburgh! There are lots of amazing attractions here to keep you both occupied including a mirror maze, vortex tunnel and a rooftop terrace with jaw-dropping views of Edinburgh.

Budget-friendly finds...

The Royal Mile
EH1 1QS

Running through the heart of Edinburgh's old town, The Royal Mile connects the iconic Edinburgh Castle to the marvellous Holyrood Palace. The mile is lined with historical sites, fabulous shops and cosy pubs & eateries (*some of the city's very best*). A couples weekend in Edinburgh isn't complete with a wonder down the Royal Mile.

Free Walking Tours
Address depends on chosen tour

There's a huge selection of free walking tours in Edinburgh – a great way to explore the city and learn about its history. Edinburgh Free Tour is popular 'classic', or why not try 'The Potter Trail' a free walking tour for you to discover magical locations that inspired characters and scenes in the series.

Our visit to Edinburgh...

We visited...

☐ Red Bus Bistro

☐ Dominion Cinema

☐ Edinburgh Castle

☐ Free Walking Tours

☐ The Royal Mile

☐ ....

☐ ....

☐ The Scotch Whisky Experience

☐ Hike to Arthur's Seat

☐ Camera Obscura & World of Illusions

☐ The Real Mary King's Close

☐ ....

☐ ....

☐ ....

Notes...

....

....

....

....

....

....

Rating: ♡ ♡ ♡ ♡ ♡

*Our favourite photo
from the weekend*

Date:

Location:

Caption:

Glasgow

Best For: Museums, live music, shopping, football & whisky.

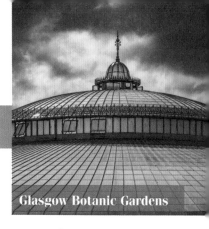

Glasgow Botanic Gardens

Scotland's biggest city: Glasgow - often referred to as one of the world's friendliest cities, is sure to keep you both smiling. Inundated with striking Victorian architecture, this vibrant city is known to be one of the most exciting in Europe. It has endless museums, art galleries and unique attractions complimented by a lively selection of music venues, pubs, bars and restaurants. Scotch enthusiasts will appreciate the numerous whisky distilleries in the city.

Romance ♥♥♥♡♡
Food & Drink ♥♥♥♡♡
Things To See ♥♥♥♡♡
Natural Beauty ♥♥♥♡♡

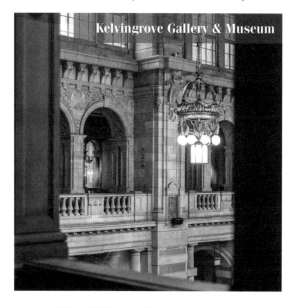

Kelvingrove Gallery & Museum

Drive Time to Glasgow
From London | 7.5 hours
From Manchester | 4 hours
From Newcastle | 3 hours
From Birmingham | 5 hours
From Cardiff | 7 hours

Train Duration to Glasgow
From London | 5 hours
From Manchester | 3.5 hours
From Newcastle | 3.5 hours
From Birmingham | 4.5 hours
From Cardiff | 7 hours

Best Time to Visit...
Summer (June-August) - Long days and a higher chance of avoiding the infamous Scottish weather (rain) – you may even experience some sunshine! With Summer, comes an abundance of festivals, but higher prices too.

December - If you can brave the Scottish weather, then this is a perfect time to come and enjoy the wide range of Christmas markets that pop up across the city. Be sure to grab a mulled wine to keep your heart and hands warm!

Best Places to Eat & Drink...

Kember & Jones | Good coffee and a sweet or savoury breakfast
134 Byres Rd, Glasgow G12 8TD

Paesano | Artisan wood-fired pizza
94 Miller St, Glasgow G1 1DT

Stravaigin | Seasonal Scottish small plates & Sunday roasts
28 Gibson St, Glasgow G12 8NX

Ubiqutious Chip | Excellent Scottish food in a unique scenic space
12 Ashton Ln, Hillhead, Glasgow G12 8SJ

Glaschu Restaurant & Bar | Fine dining in the heart of Glasgow
32 Royal Exchange Square, Glasgow G1 3AB

Top Tip: Pack a brolly or raincoat no matter what the season. Glasgow is known as one of the 'rainiest' cities in the UK, with an average of 170.3 rain days per year.

Glasgow Cathedral

Accommodation

£

The Z Hotel Glasgow | 0141 212 4550
36 North Frederick Street, Glasgow G1 2BS

Point A Glasgow | 0141 352 2650
80 Bath Street, Glasgow G2 2EN

Motel One | 0141 468 0450
82 Oswald St, Glasgow G1 4PL

££

Dakota Glasgow | 0141 404 3680
179 W Regent St, Glasgow G2 4DP

Apex City of Glasgow Hotel | 0141 375 3333
110 Bath St, Glasgow G2 2EN

Hampton by Hilton Glasgow Central | 0141 428 4441
140 W Campbell St, Glasgow G2 4TZ

£££

Kimpton Blythswood Square Hotel | 0141 248 8888
11 Blythswood Square, Glasgow G2 4AD

Alamo Guest House | 0141 339 2395
46 Gray St, Kelvingrove, Glasgow G3 7SE

15Glasgow | 0141 332 1263
15 Woodside Pl, Glasgow G3 7QL

A Weekend Itinerary...

Day	Morning	Afternoon	Evening
Friday	Arrive in Glasgow	Explore the Scottish Football Museum or the Riverside Museum	Try out Axe Hurling at Hatchet Harry's
Saturday	Visit Glasgow Cathedral & The Necropolis	Take a tour at the Clydeside Distillery	Catch a show at the Barrowland Ballroom
Sunday	Visit Kelvingrove Park and Gallery & Museum	Explore Barras Market	Travel home

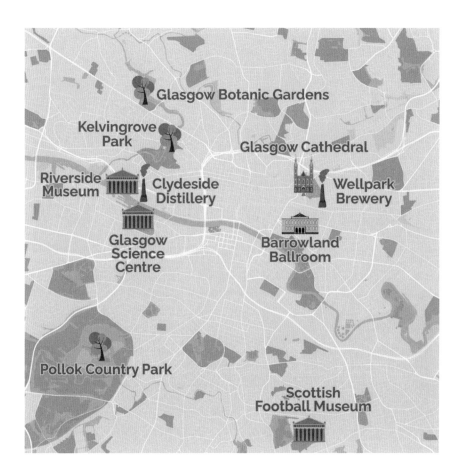

Best way to explore Glasgow...

Glasgow city centre is compact allowing you to easily get around on foot; however, some of the attractions are slightly out of the centre. Therefore, the subway is the most efficient and affordable way to explore, zipping you around Glasgow in no time at all.

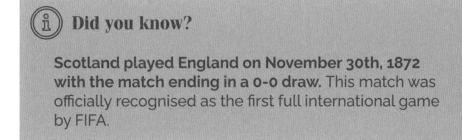

ⓘ **Did you know?**

Scotland played England on November 30th, 1872 with the match ending in a 0-0 draw. This match was officially recognised as the first full international game by FIFA.

Top picks for slowing down...

Kelvingrove Park
Park Terrace, G3 6BY

The perfect way to escape the hustle and bustle of the city! Situated next to the River Kelvin, the park is an ideal place to put your feet up, watch the world go by and maybe even enjoy a picnic *(weather permitting)*. Why not explore the Kelvingrove Art Gallery & Museum that's conveniently located within the park.

Unique things to see & do...

The Clydeside Distillery
100 Stobcross Road, G3 8QQ

Can you really go to Scotland without sampling some of its famous whisky? Learn about the traditional methods used to make the single malt scotch whisky and sample several options in the tasting room. Top tip, opt for the chocolate and whisky tasting experience, this is a great compromise if the other half isn't a huge whisky lover.

Barrowland Ballroom
244 Gallowgate, G4 0TT

Fancy an evening of live music? Head to the Barrowland Ballroom *(described as Scotland's most iconic live music venue)* and enjoy a fun-filled music inspired evening together. Purchase tickets for your preferred show online. The building is also home to street-level halls that are used for weekend markets.

Scottish Football Museum
Hampden Park, G42 9BA

You might not both be into football; however, a trip to Europe's first National Football Museum may intrigue both of you. Situated within Hampden Park *(the home of the Scottish National Team)*, there's thousands of displays for you to marvel at. If your timing's right, you might even be able to grab tickets to watch a game!

Barras Market
244 Gallowgate, G1 5DX

Barras Market is the ideal place to have a wee mooch about and you'll maybe even bag a souvenir. From bric-a-brac to antiques, this ever-popular weekend market will allow you to find something weird and wonderful. Feeling hungry? You'll find plenty of street food stalls offering a range of world cuisines.

River Clyde

Glasgow City

Kelvingrove Park

Top picks for adventure seekers...

Hatchet Harry's Axe Hurling
95 Union Street, G1 3TA

Ever thrown an axe? It's an extremely fun activity to try together! Why not challenge your partner to see who has the best technique? If you're feeling confident, the experts will even teach you how to do a trick shot! You're guaranteed to be leaving here with a smile on your face (and a bit of an aching arm!).

Escape Reality Glasgow
Basement Unit 1 (inside of Merchant Square), G1 1LE

Feeling up for a challenge? Compete as a team to escape one of the 5 rooms within this immersive experience. Be sure to bring your A-Game as you tackle a series of puzzles and challenges to escape within the 60-minute time limit. Escape rooms are a go-to couples weekend activity, just remember though, it's only a game!

Budget-friendly finds...

Glasgow Cathedral & The Necropolis
Castle Street, G4 0UZ

Glasgow's medieval Cathedral offers some of the very finest architecture in Glasgow. It's also completely free to visit. After admiring the 800-year-old building, head to the nearby Necropolis - a Victorian hill-side cemetery, offering picturesque views across Glasgow and the surrounding area.

Riverside Museum
100 Pointhouse Road, Govan, G3 8RS

Ponder around this award-winning museum of transport and travel - there's lots to see! Climb aboard an old train, tram, bus and even a restored Victorian ship (which is docked on the banks of the River Clyde). Feeling romantic? Why not head to the bow to re-enact the famous Titanic scene.

Glasgow Botanic Gardens
730 Great Western Road, G12 0UE

Take a wander around this 27-acre park and discover its woodland, gardens and walking trails. Step inside the Victorian glasshouses, including Kibble Palace, where you can admire the parks collection of tropical plants. Head to the tearoom for a cuppa and cake. Guided tours are available on Saturdays.

Our visit to Glasgow...

We visited...

☐ Kelvingrove Park

☐ Barrowland Ballroom

☐ Barras Market

☐ Escape Reality Glasgow

☐ Riverside Museum

☐ ....

☐ ....

☐ The Clydeside Distillery

☐ Scottish Football Museum

☐ Glasgow Cathedral & The Necropolis

☐ Glasgow Botanic Gardens

☐ Hatchet Harry's Axe Hurling

☐ ....

☐ ....

Notes...

....

....

....

....

....

....

Rating: ♡♡♡♡♡

*Our favourite photo
from the weekend*

Date:

Location:

Caption:

North East

Newcastle

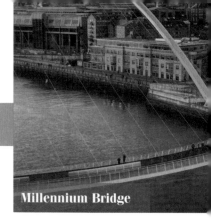

Often touted as the UK's best nightlife destination, Newcastle boasts an exceptional number of boujee bars, hip clubs, and mouth-watering food spots. Now if that doesn't tickle your fancy, fear not, there's much more to Newcastle than boozy weekends away. The city is packed with rich history, vast culture, and some phenomenal architecture. Popular spots to explore include Newcastle Castle (*a mouthful, isn't it?*), Gateshead Quayside, Grainger Market and The Victoria Tunnels. No matter what you decide to get up to, Newcastle is a canny couple's destination!

Millennium Bridge

Romance ♥♥♥♡♡
Food & Drink ♥♥♥♥♥
Things To See ♥♥♥♥♡
Natural Beauty ♥♥♡♡♡

Drive Time to Newcastle
From London | 5.5 hours
From Manchester | 3 hours
From Birmingham | 4 hours
From Cardiff | 6 hours
From Plymouth | 7.5 hours

Train Duration to Newcastle
From London | 3 hours
From Manchester | 2 hours
From Birmingham | 2 hours
From Cardiff | 6 hours
From Plymouth | 7.5 hours

Newcastle Castle

Best Time to Visit...
Newcastle is less than 50 miles from Scotland so expect cold and wet weather. The summer hot months are your best chance for drier weather. The city is buzzing when the Newcastle Utd football team play at home.

Best Places to Eat & Drink...

Francesca's Pizzeria | Italian known for its 'half pizza half pasta dish'
134-136 Manor House Rd, Jesmond NE2 2NA

Leila Lilys | Eatery & cocktails set in a boujee flower-adorned space
2-12, Grey St, Newcastle NE1 6AE

By The River Brew Co | Brewpub inside repurposed shipping containers
Hillgate Quays, Gateshead NE8 2FD

Khai Khai | Delicious Indian cuisine set in Victorian dining rooms
29 Queen St, Newcastle NE1 3UG

House of Tides | Michelin star dining with exceptional tasting menu
28-30 Close, Newcastle NE1 3RF

Top Tip: Take a stroll along the Gateshead Millennium Bridge (the world's first and only tilting bridge), it's a great way to view the River Tyne and its seven bridges!

River Tyne

Cool Bars in Newcastle...

We've added in some extra places to head for a drink as there are so many cool spots to enjoy a tipple or two; whether that be a cocktail at Mother Mercy or a pint and some live music at The Cluny.

W.C Newcastle | A Victorian toilet built in the 1800's now repurposed into one of Newcastle's best kept secrets (**yes, it's now a bar**)
High Bridge - WC, Newcastle NE1 1UW

The Holy Hobo | Midday lunchin' to discos & brunchin'. Another quirky bar with punchy cocktails, tasty food and music
THREE, Jesmond Three Sixty, Newcastle NE2 1DB

Twenty Twenty | 20 Signature Cocktails and 20" Pizzas! Top rated...
5 Bigg Market, Newcastle NE1 1UN

Mother Mercy | Voted one of the UK's Top 50 Cocktail Bars
The Old George Yard, 44 Cloth Market, Newcastle NE1 1EE

The Cluny | The place to head for live music with a warm welcome
36 Lime St, Newcastle NE1 2PQ

FOLLOW US ON INSTAGRAM

@NOFUSSTRAVELGUIDES

FOR TRAVEL TIPS, PHOTOS & MORE!

SCAN ME

NO✈FUSS
TRAVEL GUIDES

Accommodation

Travelodge Newcastle Central | 0871 984 6164
Forster Street, Quayside, Newcastle NE1 2NH

Holiday Inn Express Gateshead | 0371 902 1625
Clasper Way, Newcastle NE16 3BE

Staybridge Suites Newcastle | 0191 238 7000
Buxton Street, Newcastle NE1 6NL

Hampton by Hilton Newcastle | 0191 500 5001
Baron House Neville Street, Newcastle NE1 5EN

Motel One Newcastle | 0191 211 109
15-25 High Bridge, Newcastle NE1 1EW

Malmaison Newcastle | 0191 389 8627
Quayside, Newcastle NE1 3DX

INNSiDE by Meliá Newcastle | 0191 338 7710
River View, Close Bridge Court, Newcastle NE1 3BE

Jesmond Dene House | 0191 212 3000
Jesmond Dene Rd, Newcastle NE2 2EY

Hilton Newcastle Gateshead | 0191 490 9700
Bottle Bank, Gateshead NE8 2AR

A Weekend Itinerary...

Day	Morning	Afternoon	Evening
Friday	Arrive in Newcastle	Explore Newcastle City Centre and Shopping Centre	Dinner at Twenty Twenty & a cabaret show at Boulevard
Saturday	Explore Newcastle Castle & Newcastle Cathedral	Take a tour of the Victoria Tunnel or wander around Grainger Market	Dinner at Pizzeria Francesca & Drinks and Music at The Holy Hobo
Sunday	Quayside Sunday Market	Baltic Centre & By The River Brew Co for Lunch	Travel home

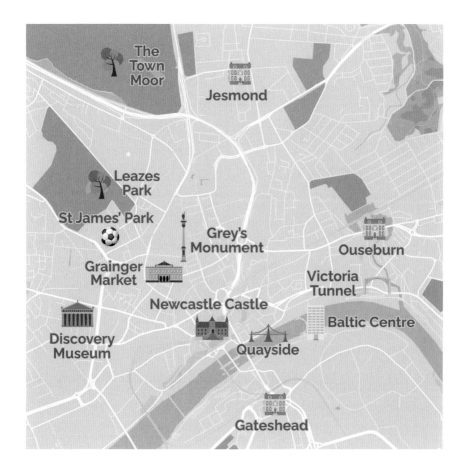

Best way to explore Newcastle...

Newcastle's main attractions are generally within walking distance. For everything else, The Tyne & Wear Metro system is excellent. A single ticket costs around £4.30 and an all-zone Metro Daysaver with unlimited travel costs around £6.20. For those more adventurous, you can hire Neuron E-Scooters to whizz around.

 Did you know?

Newcastle is home to the first ever branch of the high street bakery Greggs (thanks to local John Gregg), and currently has the highest number of branches in any UK city with over 30 branches!

Top picks for slowing down...

The City Baths Newcastle
Northumberland Road, NE1 8SG

A relaxing visit to the recently refurbished Turkish Baths offer a delightful spa experience for those looking to unwind. A 2-hour session including access to the Turkish Baths, Sauna and Pool offers the best value. If you're looking for the complete spa experience, there are a number of Spa Treatments available.

Toon Tour Open Top Bus
Neville Street, NE1 5DL

Looking for a more relaxing way to explore the city? This open bus tour has 17 stops to explore including the popular Ouseburn, Quayside, St James' Park and more. The bus runs every 30 minutes from 10:05am to 16:05pm at Central station. Please note, the tours only operate from the end of May until the start of October.

Unique things to see & do...

Victoria Tunnel Tour
Ouse St, NE1 2PF

The Victoria Tunnel Tour provides an hour and a quarter of spellbinding storytelling, fascinating history, and plenty of laughter. Ranging from the Victorian era when it was first constructed to World War II, you'll discover all of the tunnel's stories and secrets. This is a great shout for you curious cats. Book online.

Boulevard
3-9 Churchill Street, NE1 4HF

A wild card location! Boulevard is the city's number one cabaret venue. Prepare yourself for spectacular choreography, dazzling costumes and side-splitting comedy. We've got a feeling you're both going to love this place. Tickets prices vary depending on your seating area. Shows every Friday & Saturday evening.

Newcastle City

Quayside

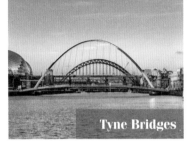

Tyne Bridges

Baltic Centre

Top picks for culture seekers...

Newcastle Castle
The Black Gate, Castle Garth, NE1 1RQ

A castle in Newcastle, who'd have thought it eh? Steeped in history, the adventurous side in you will enjoy exploring the ancient passageways and chambers of this Norman fortress. A journey to the roof will provide excellent views of the city. Pre-book tickets online or pay on the day.

Baltic Centre for Contemporary Art
South Shore Road, Gateshead, NE8 3BA

Located on Quayside in a converted mill, the Baltic Centre is the biggest gallery of its kind in the world. If art galleries aren't your usual go to then fear not, it's free to enter so there's nothing to lose. There's a café, shop and the restaurant located on Baltic's iconic rooftop offers stunning city views.

The Discovery Museum
Blandford Square, NE1 4JA

A huge space showcasing the best of the area's heritage over three floors crammed with extensive galleries of inventions, world-firsts, model ships and interactive activities. Another free to enter location, you'll both learn the story of Newcastle and its people from Roman times through to the present day.

Budget-friendly finds...

Grainger Market
Grainger Street, NE1 5QQ

First opened in 1835, Grainger Market has mix of traditional stalls, local vendors & some epic street food options. You'll find almost everything you can imagine here and like most of Newcastle, it's reasonably priced. Just a short 2-minute walk from the market is the Grey's Monument, a definite must see.

Quayside
S Shore Road, Gateshead NE8 3BA

Did you really go to Newcastle without a stroll along the mighty Quayside? Newcastle and Gateshead are separated by the River Tyne which is straddled by several iconic bridges. Take a romantic walk along Quayside, quench your thirst in any of its pubs & bars. Visit on a Sunday to explore the Quayside Market.

Our visit to Newcastle...

We visited...

☐ The City Baths

☐ Victoria Tunnel Tour

☐ Newcastle Castle

☐ The Discovery Museum

☐ Quayside

☐ ....

☐ ....

☐ Toon Tour Open Top Bus

☐ Boulevard

☐ Baltic Centre for Contemporary Art

☐ Grainger Market

☐ ....

☐ ....

☐ ....

Notes...

....

....

....

....

....

....

Rating: ♡♡♡♡♡

*Our favourite photo
from the weekend*

Date:

Location:

Caption:

Durham

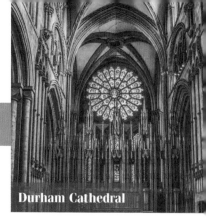

Durham Cathedral

A historic city with roots all the way back to the Roman Empire. Durham combines iconic landmarks with modern advancements and is surrounded by natural beauty. From discovering the history behind the city's famous cathedral and castle to digging into some delicious dishes and even ghost hunting *(with ghostbusting equipment, no less)*, Durham is full of fun and surprises.

Romance ♥♥♥♥♡
Food & Drink ♥♥♥♡♡
Things To See ♥♥♥♥♡
Natural Beauty ♥♥♥♥♡

Durham City

Drive Time to Durham
From London | 5 hours
From Manchester | 2.5 hours
From Newcastle | 0.5 hour
From Birmingham | 3.5 hours
From Cardiff | 5.5 hours

Train Duration to Durham
From London | 3 hours
From Manchester | 2 hours
From Newcastle | 0.5 hour
From Birmingham | 3 hours
From Cardiff | 6 hours

Best Time to Visit...
Summer - May through to August will give you both maximum daylight and the best weather to explore Durham and its surrounding areas. Keep in mind it will be a bit busier during the school holidays!
Winter - Visit Durham during the most magical time of year and take in its annual Christmas festival and its markets.

Best Places to Eat & Drink...

Tealicious Tearoom | Friendly tea and brunch spot
88 Elvet Bridge, Durham DH1 3AG

Zen | Family-owned Thai restaurant
Court Lane, Durham DH1 3JS

La Spada Ristorante | A slice of Italy in the heart of Durham
62-64 Front Street, Durham DH1 5DE

Restaurant 17 | Delicious dishes made by local produce
17 Elvet Bridge, Durham DH1 3AA

Coarse | Michelin-star fine dining
Reform Pl, North Rd, Durham DH1 4RZ

Top Tip: Head to Market Place to discover the best architecture in the city, as well as an array of independent stores within Durham Market Hall. For boutique stores head to Fowlers Yard.

Durham City

Accommodation

£

Radisson Blu Hotel Durham | 0191 372 7200
Frankland Lane, Durham DH1 5TA

The Victoria Inn | 0191 386 5269
86 Hallgarth Street, Durham DH1 3AS

The Honest Lawyer Hotel | 0191 378 3780
Croxdale, Durham DH1 3SP

££

Hotel Indigo Durham | 0808 169 7530
Old Shire Hall 9 Old Elvet, Durham DH1 3HL

Castle View Guest House | 0191 386 8852
4 Crossgate, Durham DH1 4PS

The Kingslodge Inn | 0191 370 9977
Waddington Street Flass Vale, Durham DH1 4BG

£££

40 Winks Guest House | 0191 380 3000
40 South Street, Durham DH1 4QP

Durham Riverside Apartments | 0780 960 1955
St. Andrews Court New Elvet, Durham DH1 3AH

The Townhouse Durham | 0191 359 2440
34 Old Elvet, Durham DH1 3HN

A Weekend Itinerary...

Day	Morning	Afternoon	Evening
Friday	Arrive in Durham	Take a tour of Durham Castle	Enjoy a show at the Magic Corner
Saturday	Explore Durham Cathedral	Take a stroll around Crook Hall Gardens	Dinner at Coarse
Sunday	Bounce around at Infinite Air	Brunch at Tealicious Tearoom	Travel home

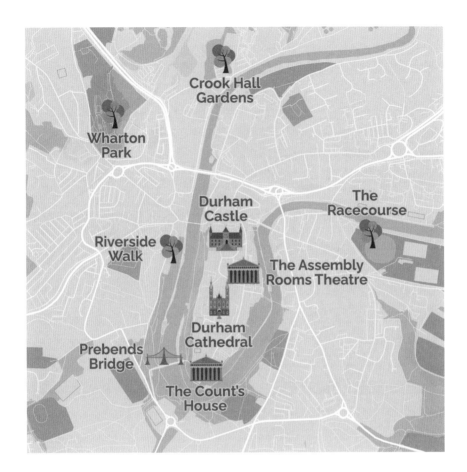

Best way to explore Durham...

Durham is certainly a walkable city; just be aware it is quite hilly and made of many cobbled streets so pack sensible footwear. Being a university city, there are also quite regular bus services running within the city.

 Did you know?

You can't get more British than English mustard and Durham claims to be the home of the beloved condiment. One Mrs Clement decided to grind up her mustard seeds to spice up her dishes. It took off across the UK and was eventually bought by Colman's of Norwich.

Top picks for slowing down...

The Magic Corner
19½, Old Elvet, DH1 3HL

Prepare to be wowed by magician Tom Bolton at the Magic Corner, a custom-built 'Magic Show Bar' in the heart of Durham. During an immersive, close-up show you'll both be shown seemingly impossible tricks and illusions. You'll want to get your tickets well in advance as shows book up very quickly here!

The Assembly Rooms Theatre
40 N Bailey, DH1 3ET

A 175-seater venue found in the historic North Bailey area. Showcasing both the University of Durham performances and professional productions, there's a show for everyone – including cabaret, musicals and dramas. Check out the venue's website to see what's on and get your tickets there.

Unique things to see & do...

Durham Castle Tour
Palace Green, DH1 3RW

Once an imposing fortress, Durham Castle is now home to the students of University College, part of Durham University. With over 1,000 years of history, it's a must-visit for history lovers where you'll both uncover the castle's deepest secrets. Entry is via a 50-minute guided tour only, which we recommend booking in advance.

Durham Cathedral
The College, DH1 3EH

Calling all Harry Potter fans! You might get a sense of déjà vu when exploring the iconic Grade I listed building, which was used to recreate Hogwarts during the first and second HP films. Head to a transfiguration class with Professor McGonagall in the Chapter House or recreate Ron's 'eat slugs' blunder in the Cloister Garth!

Durham Ghost Walk
Durham City Centre, DH1

Are you both brave enough to take on the ghosts of Durham? Join Durham Ghost Walk, where you'll be shown the most haunted areas of the city. Armed with ghost-hunting machines (*yep, that's right*) there are several tours on offer – including an adults-only one where you'll learn about plenty of spooky but spicy past deeds!

Durham Cathedral

Top picks for adventure seekers...

Infinite Air
Belmont Industrial Estate,
DH1 1GG

With a tagline of 'Extreme Trampoline' you can be
sure a trip to Infinite Air is going to be a fun-filled one.
After taking on the inflatable assault courses, dunking
in the basketball hoops and generally bouncing to
your heart's content, treat yourselves at the Lickety
Split Ice Cream Parlour!

Adventure Access
Unit 1a, The Castleside,
Seaham Harbour Marina,
Seaham SR7 7EY

Located just under 15 miles from Durham city centre in
the coastal town of Seaham, Adventure Access CIC offers
a range of fun activities out on the water. These include
stand up paddleboarding through Durham, kayaking and
even dragonboating! As it's located a little outside the city,
you'll want to book ahead to avoid disappointment.

Budget-friendly finds...

Oriental Museum
Elvet Hill Road, South Road,
DH1 3TH

Through Ancient Egypt all the way to modern-day
China, Durham's Oriental Museum showcases the art
and history of the cultures of both Asia and Northern
Africa. Free to visit, plan to spend around two hours
taking in all the exhibitions and enjoy a cuppa and
some cake at the café.

Crook Hall Gardens
Frankland Lane, Sidegate,
DH1 5SZ

Take a romantic, leisurely stroll together in the historic
Crook Hall Gardens and explore its beautiful landscapes and abundant wildlife. Now owned by the
National Trust, the 10-acre gardens are home to an
orchard, a hedge maze and a second hand bookshop
– what more could you want!

Our visit to Durham...

We visited...

☐ The Magic Corner

☐ Durham Cathedral

☐ Durham Ghost Walk

☐ Adventure Access

☐ Crook Hall Gardens

☐ ....

☐ ....

☐ Durham Castle Tour

☐ Infinite Air

☐ The Assembly Rooms Theatre

☐ Oriental Museum

☐ ....

☐ ....

☐ ....

Notes...

....

....

....

....

....

....

Rating: ♡ ♡ ♡ ♡ ♡

*Our favourite photo
from the weekend*

Date:

Location:

Caption:

North West

Lake District

Arguably England's most beautiful corner! A wholesome weekend in the Lakes is the ultimate couple's getaway. Forget your busy life back home, turn on your out of office and escape to this magical National Park filled with captivating landscapes, bustling market towns and wonderful outdoor pursuits. The Lake District is relatively large, so to make things easier, we've based most of our suggestions on the area around Windermere *(a perfect base to explore from)*.

Honister Pass

Romance ♥♥♥♥♡
Food & Drink ♥♥♥♡♡
Things To See ♥♥♥♥♡
Natural Beauty ♥♥♥♥♥

Coniston

Drive Time to Windermere
From London | 5 hours
From Manchester | 1.5 hours
From Newcastle | 2 hours
From Birmingham | 3 hours
From Cardiff | 4.5 hours

Train Duration to Windermere
From London | 3 hours
From Manchester | 1.5 hours
From Newcastle | 2.5 hours
From Birmingham | 2.5 hours
From Cardiff | 4.5 hours

Best Time to Visit...
The Lakes are busiest in July & August when the weather also tends to be better. Visit in the Spring or Autumn where you'll be avoiding most of the crowds. The weather can change quickly all year round.

Best Places to Eat & Drink...

Steam Bistro | Breakfast, brunch and relaxed all day lunches
Tilberthwaite Avenue, Coniston LA21 8ED

Boardwalk Bar & Grill | Lakeside views & wholesome food
Gilly's Landing, Glebe Rd, Windermere LA23 3HE

Afternoon Tea at Cedar Manor | A delightful afternoon tea experience!
Ambleside Road, Windermere LA23 1AX

Tacos Del Sol | Authentic Mexican Street food
2a Cheapside, Ambleside LA22 0AB

Mrs F's Fine Food Emporium | Quirky café - scones, toasties & pies!
74 Main Street, Keswick CA12 5DX

Top Tip: Make sure you pack your walking boots, you're going to need them - and your raincoats, you're likely to need those too! The weather is usually wet and mild most of the year.

Windermere

Accommodation

£

Melbourne Guest House | 0153 944 3475
3 Biskey Howe Rd, Windermere LA23 2JP

Craigholme | 0153 944 8309
70 Craig Walk, Bowness-on-Windermere LA23 2JS

Compston House B & B | 0153 943 2305
Compston Road, Ambleside LA22 9DJ

££

The Royal Oak Inn | 0153 944 3970
Brantfell Rd, Bowness-on-Windermere LA23 3EG

The Ro Hotel | 0153 923 2625
15-25 Helm Rd, Bowness-on-Windermere LA23 3BA

The Ruddings | 0176 877 8436
Braithwaite, Keswick, CA12 5RY

£££

Aphrodites Boutique Suites | 0153 944 5052
Longtail Hill, Bowness on Windermere LA23 3JD

Storrs Hall | 0153 944 7111
Bowness-on-Windermere LA23 3LG

Lodore Falls Hotel & Spa | 0330 056 4880
B5289, Keswick CA12 5UX

A Weekend Itinerary...

Day	Morning	Afternoon	Evening
Friday	Arrive in the Lake District	Explore the World of Beatrix Potter Attraction	Relax at the Low Wood Bay Spa (3 hour session from 4pm)
Saturday	Hop onboard a Windermere Lake Cruise	Explore the Orrest Head Walk	Dinner & drinks at Boardwalk Bar & Grill
Sunday	Enjoy the Winder-mere Circular Drive	Take on the Infinity Bridge at Honister	Travel home

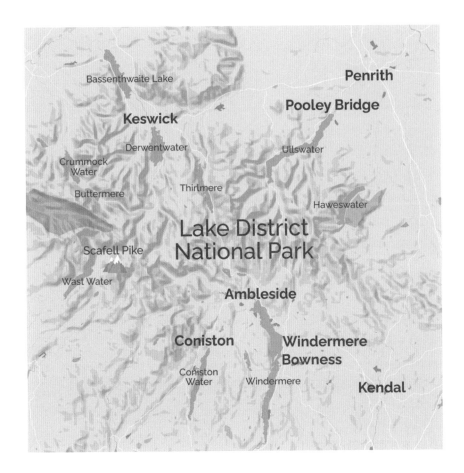

Best way to explore the Lake District...

Getting around the Lakes is most convenient with your own vehicle. If you don't drive, fear not, the bus network will get you to and from the major destinations including Windermere, Keswick & Kendal no problem. If you arrive by train, change at Oxenholme Lake District to pick up the short line to Windermere. We'd recommend using Bowness or Windermere as a base if you don't have your own vehicle.

 Did you know?

There is only one official lake in the Lake District, which is Bassenthwaite Lake. Bassenthwaite is the only one to have the word 'lake' in its title. The rest are regarded as 'tarns', 'meres' or 'waters.'

Top picks for slowing down...

Windermere Lake Cruises

Bowness Pier, Glebe Road,
Bowness-on-Windermere
LA23 3HE

Enjoy the spectacular views of England's longest lake on board a Windermere Lake Cruise. Not only are the cruises a perfect lazy way to explore the area, but they also offer a hop-on / hop-off service allowing you to visit Brockhole, Ambleside & Lakeside *(home to the Lakes Aquarium)*. They also offer self-drive options.

Low Wood Bay Spa

Ambleside Road, Windermere
LA23 1LP

Take in views of Windermere whilst you soak in the heated outdoor infinity pool - the ideal way to unwind on your weekend away. They have a wide range of both indoor & outdoor thermal spaces including outdoor hot tubs perfect for early evening star gazing. Several spa packages & treatments are available.

Unique things to see & do...

The World of Beatrix Potter Attraction

Bowness-on-Windermere
LA23 3BX

The World of Beatrix Potter Attraction celebrates everything about Beatrix Potter - the English author and illustrator who is best known for her imaginative children's books *(the most famous of all being The Tale of Peter Rabbit)*. Bookworms, nostalgia seekers and those looking for a rainy-day escape should head here.

Walking with Wolves - Predator Experience

Ayside, Grange-over-Sands
LA11 6HY

An experience you won't forget! You'll be doing exactly what it says on the tin on the 'Walk with Wolves Experience'. The expert handler will guide you through all aspects of evolution, physiology, social structure, communication, and conservation of the Wolf. A very highly rated experience that was featured on BBC 1's Countryfile!

Orrest Head

Honister Pass

Windermere

Ambleside

Top picks for adventure seekers...

Gorge Scrambling in Coniston
Lake Road, Coniston
LA21 8AN

An incredibly fun, thrilling and rewarding activity! Gorge/Ghyll Scrambling involves plunge pool jumping, waterfall climbs and swimming through deep rock pools as you follow one of the many streams, becks and gorges. All equipment is provided. Look for Adventure 21 where you'll explore the Coniston Coppermines.

Cumbrian Kayaking
Brockhole, Windermere
LA23 1FF

An epic kayaking adventure on Windermere! All equipment is provided, and you'll be able to soak in the views of Wansfell, Loughrigg, Claife Heights and Scandale Horseshoe from the water. There will be no crowds of tourists, no sounds of boat motors, just you, your other half, your paddle, and that view. Pre-book online.

Honister Slate Mine
Honister Pass, Keswick
CA12 5XN

A slate mine may sound quite tame right? Trust us, it's not! Honister offers several adrenaline fuelled pursuits including the Via Ferrata Xtreme, which combines scrambling and climbing across Honister Crag *(while harnessed)* and an infinity bridge, which will test your nerve. Those with a fear of heights should avoid this one! Pre-book online.

Budget-friendly finds...

Windermere Circular Drive
Windermere, LA23 1AL

Enjoy this scenic 45'ish mile drive where you'll encounter pristine lake views, twisty mountain roads and picturesque villages. Start in Windermere, head to Ambleside then continue to Rydal, Grasmere, Dungeon Ghyll, Little Langdale, Coniston, Hawkshead, Lakeside then finally to Bowness. Don't forget a picnic or snacks for the drive!

Orrest Head Walk
Kendal Road, Windermere, LA23 1AL

This signposted route begins at the lower entrance of the Windermere Hotel, is 3.5km long and rewards adventurers with 360° views over Windermere and the central fells. If you're doubting your ability, trust us, it'll only take around 20 minutes to reach the summit and it'll be worth it! Head further North for more challenging mountain hikes.

Our visit to the Lake District...

We visited...

- ☐ Windermere Lake
- ☐ Walking with Wolves
- ☐ Honister Slate Mine
- ☐ Orrest Head Walk
- ☐ Gorge Scrambling in Coniston
- ☐ ....
- ☐ ....

- ☐ Low Wood Bay Spa
- ☐ Cumbrian Kayaking
- ☐ The World of Beatrix Potter Attraction
- ☐ Windermere Circular Drive
- ☐ ....
- ☐ ....

Notes...

....

....

....

....

....

....

Rating: ♡ ♡ ♡ ♡ ♡

*Our favourite photo
from the weekend*

Date:

Location:

Caption:

Blackpool

As one of the UK's most beloved and cherished seaside towns, Blackpool is a great getaway destination to let go and have some fun to-gether. Reclaim the innocence of childhood by taking on Blackpool Pleasure Beach's wildest rides or splash, frolic and dive into Blackpool's Sandcastle Waterpark. Evenings can be spent enjoying some raucous entertainment and the town's many cafés are perfect for a morning pick-me-up. There's certainly no shortage of fun to be had in Blackpool!

Blackpool Central Pier

Romance ♥♥♥♡♡
Food & Drink ♥♥♥♡♡
Things To See ♥♥♥♥♡
Natural Beauty ♥♥♡♡♡

Blackpool Tower

Drive Time to Blackpool
From London | 4.5 hours
From Manchester | 1 hour
From Newcastle | 3 hours
From Birmingham | 2 hours
From Cardiff | 4 hours

Train Duration to Blackpool
From London | 3 hours
From Manchester | 1.5 hours
From Newcastle | 3.5 hours
From Birmingham | 2.5 hours
From Cardiff | 4.5 hours

Best Time to Visit...
Spring - Aim to visit between late March and May to get the best chance of good weather without hordes of summer holiday-goers.
Autumn - Most rides and attractions are still up and running from September to late October without the high prices that the summer season demands.

Best Places to Eat & Drink...

CuriosiTea At 23 | Snug tea and cake café
23 Layton Road, Blackpool FY3 8EA

Yorkshire Fisheries | Traditional fish and chips
16 Topping Street, Blackpool FY1 3AQ

Hungarian's Restaurant | Authentic warming Hungarian dishes
57 Topping Street First Floor, Upstairs, Blackpool FY1 3AF

Hauze Restaurant | European menu with a cosy atmosphere
28-30 Talbot Road, Blackpool FY1 1LF

Twisted Indian Street Food | Highly regarded Indian eatery
15a Clifton Street, Blackpool FY1 1JD

> **Top Tip:** Book attractions, such as the Pleasure Beach, in advance to save money and avoid queuing. eTickets for the Pleasure Beach must be purchased before midnight the day before your visit to benefit from the pre-booking saving.

Blackpool Pleasure Beach

Accommodation

Doric Hotel | 0125 335 1751
48-52 Queens Promenade, Blackpool FY2 9RP

The Ruskin Hotel | 0125 362 4063
55-69 Albert Road, Blackpool FY1 4PW

McGraths Blackpool | 0743 220 6784
87 Lord Street, Blackpool FY1 2DG

Number One South Beach | 0125 334 3900
4 Harrowside West, Blackpool FY4 1NW

The Imperial Hotel | 0125 362 3971
North Promenade, Blackpool FY1 2HB

Park House Hotel | 0125 362 0081
308 Promenade, Blackpool FY1 2HA

Boulevard Hotel | 0125 333 6073
Ocean Boulevard Promenade, Blackpool FY4 1PL

16 Empress Drive Apartments | 0125 3713 535
16 Empress Drive, Blackpool, FY2 9SE

Queens Mansions Holiday Apartments | 0125 335 6657
224 Queens Promenade, Blackpool FY2 9HP

A Weekend Itinerary...

Day	Morning	Afternoon	Evening
Friday	Arrive in Blackpool	Blackpool Pleasure Beach	Dinner at Hauze Restaurant
Saturday	Explore Stanley Park	Visit the Blackpool Tower Dungeon	Have a laugh at the Comedy Station
Sunday	Discover Blackpool Zoo	Afternoon tea at CuriosiTea At 23	Travel home

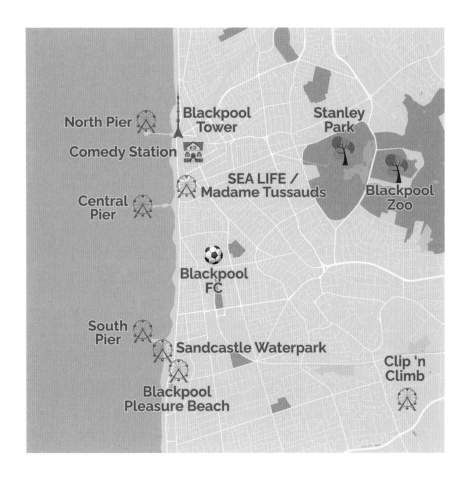

Best way to explore Blackpool...

Blackpool's attractions are spread out across the coastline but thankfully the town runs a comprehensive tram system from Starr Gate in the south all the way up to the Ferry Terminus in Fleetwood. Running every 15-30 minutes, you never have to wait long before catching a ride!

 Did you know?

The Blackpool Tower was inspired by the Eiffel Tower and was built way back in 1894. It took seven years to paint and the lift travels around 3,500 miles every year – more than the distance from Blackpool to New York!

Top picks for slowing down...

Viva Blackpool
3 Church Street, FY1 1HJ

A Las Vegas-inspired entertainment extravaganza, Viva Blackpool claims to offer the ultimate show night out. Don't expect classics or the ballet here, but there'll be plenty of fun and laughs to be had from country covers to spectacular cabaret shows. See what shows are on offer and book your tickets online.

The Comedy Station
Bank Hey Street, FY1 4RU

Priding itself on showcasing the very best that the UK stand-up scene has to offer, the Comedy Station Comedy Club has been serving up belly laughs since 2002. With big names such as Jason Manford and Eddie Izzard gracing its stage, prepare yourselves for a night of tears (the good kind!).

Unique things to see & do...

Blackpool Zoo
E Park Drive, FY3 8PP

Found within 37 acres of beautiful, open English parkland, Blackpool Zoo is a wild retreat inside the centre of the coastal town. Home to over 1,000 animals including a group of Bornean orangutans, Californian sea lions and a herd of elephants, it's a wonderful day out for all animal lovers! Book online for a saving.

The Blackpool Tower Ballroom
Blackpool Tower, Promenade, FY1 4BJ

Inside the iconic Blackpool Tower is a Gatsby-esque ballroom where you and your partner can dance the day away on its impressive mahogany, walnut and oak floor. If you forget to pack your dancing shoes, you can still enjoy the atmosphere and watch from the theatre balconies.

The Blackpool Tower Dungeon
Tower Entrance, Bank Hey Street, FY1 4BJ

Get ready for a fright-thrilled adventure through Lancashire's past at the Blackpool Tower Dungeon. With a host of theatrical actors, special effects, stages and an exhilarating ride packed into one wild experience, it's equal parts scary and fun. Pre-booking your tickets online is essential.

Blackpool North Pier

Blackpool Seafront

Top picks for adventure seekers...

Sandcastle Waterpark
Promenade, FY4 1BB

Rediscover the child-like glee of zipping down slides and taking on wild wave pools together at Blackpool's Sandcastle Waterpark. After an hour or so enjoying the water, head to the adults-only 'Sea Breeze Spa' to unwind in the steam room, sauna, aromatherapy room, salt inhalation room and heat loungers.

Blackpool Pleasure Beach
525 Ocean Blvd, FY4 1EZ

For adrenaline-junkie couples, there aren't many better UK coastal theme parks to visit than the award-winning Blackpool Pleasure Beach. Take on ICON, the UK's first double-launch roller coaster or hold onto your stomachs on The Big One! Please note, most rides close in the winter but are replaced by Christmas activities.

Clip 'n Climb Blackpool
Apollo Court, FY4 5FS

An indoor climbing experience like no other, Clip 'n Climb Blackpool combines climbing walls with theme park fun. With 20 individual and multi-climber wall challenges, your and your partner's agility, strength and courage will all be put to the test. Make sure to arrive at least 15 minutes before your slot for a safety briefing.

Budget-friendly finds...

Stanley Park
West Park Drive, FY3 9HQ

Escape into a green haven at Stanley Park, a Grade II listed park that opened in 1926. With 390 acres of beautiful landscape to explore, it's the perfect spot for a quiet, romantic walk. Open from dawn to dusk every day of the year, Stanley Park is a must-visit for all outdoorsy couples.

Our visit to Blackpool...

We visited...

☐ Viva Blackpool

☐ Blackpool Zoo

☐ Sandcastle Waterpark

☐ Clip 'n Climb Blackpool

☐ Stanley Park

☐ ....

☐ ....

☐ The Comedy Station

☐ The Blackpool Tower Ballroom

☐ Blackpool Pleasure Beach

☐ The Blackpool Tower Dungeon

☐ ....

☐ ....

☐ ....

Notes...

....

....

....

....

....

....

Rating: ♡♡♡♡♡

*Our favourite photo
from the weekend*

Date:

Location:

Caption:

Manchester

An iconic cultural hub for the North West, Manchester has it all – a storied past, a thriving present and a very exciting future. Home to Oasis, two of the biggest footy clubs globally and a leading art scene, Manchester is the king of cool. With its extensive selection of 'mint' eateries, theatres and independent shops, it's the perfect weekend city getaway for you and your significant other.

Northern Quarter

Romance ♥♥♥♡♡
Food & Drink ♥♥♥♥♥
Things To See ♥♥♥♡♡
Natural Beauty ♥♥♡♡♡

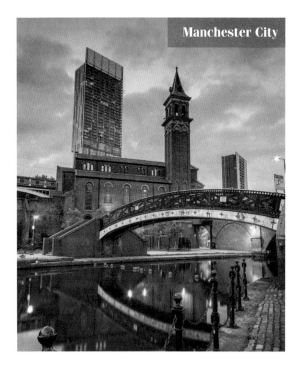

Manchester City

Drive Time to Manchester
From London | 4 hours
From Newcastle | 1 hour
From Birmingham | 2 hours
From Cardiff | 3.5 hours
From Plymouth | 5.5 hours

Train Duration to Manchester
From London | 2.5 hours
From Newcastle | 1 hour
From Birmingham | 1.5 hours
From Cardiff | 3.5 hours
From Plymouth | 5.5 hours

Best Time to Visit...
Spring - If you prefer to avoid crowds where possible, visit between March and May when the weather is fairly predictable *(pack an umbrella, just in case!)* and the tourism levels are still quite low.
Summer - With the longer days you'll both have more time to explore Manchester and all it has to offer.

Best Places to Eat & Drink...

Moose Coffee | Tasty, affordable breakfast spot
20 York Street, Manchester M2 3BB

Café North | Welcoming family-run café
66 Shudehill Northern Quarter, Manchester M4 4AA

Vincenzo Trattoria | A cosy Italian restaurant
368 Barlow Moor Road Chorlton, Manchester M21 8AZ

The Blues Kitchen Manchester | Drinks, food & live music
13 Quay Street, Manchester M3 3HN

mana | One-star Michelin restaurant serving inventive dishes
42 Blossom Street, Manchester M4 6BF

Top Tip: Manchester operates a free bus service around the city centre, take advantage of this to save on the pennies and your legs! There are two free buses which take seperate routes around the city.

Manchester City

Extra Eateries in Manchester...

We've added in some extra eateries as there are so many good spots to enjoy delicious delicacies; whether that be a rolo cookie from Gooey or some freshly made nachos from Mackie Mayor.

Cloud 23 | Cocktail & champagne sky bar overlooking Manchester, offering afternoon tea & nibbles. Perfect for a special occasion.
Beetham Tower, 303 Deansgate, Manchester M3 4LQ

Mackie Mayor Food Hall | 9 independent and incredible kitchens & bars offering everything from tacos to steak sandwiches!
Smithfield Market Hall, 1 Eagle St, Manchester M4 5BU

Canto | Modern Mediterranean tapas in a relaxed setting.
Cutting Room Square, Blossom St, Ancoats, Manchester M4 5DH

Pot Kettle Black | Delicious coffee, brunch and cocktails.
Angel Gardens, 1 Rochdale Road, Manchester M4 4GE

Gooey | Bakery and café that's a great spot for breakfast & brunch.
103 High Street, Manchester M4 1HQ

Manchester City Centre

Accommodation

£

Motel One Manchester Royal Exchange | 0161 228 0800
Commercial Buildings 15 Cross Street, Manchester M2 1WE

Travelodge Manchester Piccadilly | 0871 984 6513
31 Piccadilly, Manchester M1 1LU

easyHotel Manchester City Centre | 0161 870 2899
33 Dale Street Bradley House, Manchester M1 2HF

££

The Cow Hollow Hotel | 0161 228 7277
57 Newton Street, Manchester M1 1ET

Leven Manchester | 0161 359 7900
40 Chorlton Street, Manchester M1 3HW

Kimpton Clocktower Hotel | 0808 178 1591
Oxford Street, Manchester M60 7HA

£££

The Edwardian Manchester | 0161 835 9929
Peter Street Peter Street, Manchester M2 5GP

CitySuites II | 0161 302 0202
1 New Kings Head Yard, Manchester M3 7GF

Hotel Gotham | 0161 413 0000
100 King Street, Manchester M2 4WU

A Weekend Itinerary...

Day	Morning	Afternoon	Evening
Friday	Arrive in Manchester	Visit Chinatown	Have a laugh at the Frog and Bucket Comedy Club
Saturday	Head for breakfast at Moose Coffee	Explore the John Rylands Library	Enjoy dinner, drinks and live music at The Blues Kitchen
Sunday	Explore the Northern Quarter	Experience axe throwing at Whistle Punks	Travel home

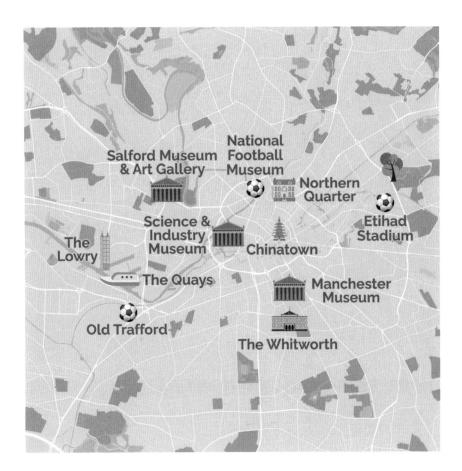

Best way to explore Manchester...

Manchester is an ever-expanding city but thanks to good public transport services, like the Metrolink and regular bus lines, it's easy to get around both in and outside of the city.

 Did you know?

Manchester's Liverpool Road Station, opened in 1830, is the world's oldest surviving railway station.
Although maybe best known for birthing the Gallagher brothers and Oasis, Manchester was also the launching pad for The Smiths and Joy Division.

Top picks for slowing down...

The Lowry
Pier, 8 The Quays, Salford, M50 3AZ

Found on the waterside at the heart of The Quays, The Lowry is a stunning, award-winning charity that houses two theatres, relaxing art galleries, cafés, bars and a restaurant. For an added slice of romance and magic, take a stroll around the waterside in the evening and watch the sun dip below the horizon.

Frog and Bucket Comedy Club
102 Oldham Street, M4 1LJ

If you're both in need of a good laugh, get down to the Frog and Bucket Comedy Club for an evening of giggles. Where Peter Kay, Johnny Vegas and Jason Manford all cut their teeth in the 90s and 00s, today it attracts some of the biggest superstars and up-and-comers in comedy.

HOME (Manchester)
2 Tony Wilson Pl, M15 4FN

Catch a movie or show at the independently run HOME (Manchester). Whether you fancy watching a Hollywood blockbuster, a rom-com or a cool indie film, you're covered here. Grab some snacks and popcorn, but make sure to save room so you can try out HOME's restaurant after the show!

Unique things to see & do...

Science and Industry Museum
Liverpool Road, M3 4JP

Showcasing Manchester's rich manufacturing history, with it being considered the first industrial city in the world, the Science and Industry Museum offers a fun and educational day out. Open 10am - 5pm on the weekends, plan to spend about around two hours exploring this museum.

John Rylands Library
150 Deansgate, M3 3EH

Perfect for couples who love history and literature, John Rylands Library is an iconic Manchester landmark. Housed in a beautiful late-Victorian neo-Gothic building, the library opened to the public in 1900. Please note, the library is open to the public from 10am to 5pm on Wednesday to Saturday each week.

Chinatown

Northern Quarter

The Lowry

Top picks for adventure seekers...

Whistle Punks Urban Axe Throwing
Great Northern Warehouse, Unit 20, Atrium level, 235 Deansgate, M3 4EN

Move over bowling, there's a new fun date night activity in town, axe throwing! You'll both be guided by an axe throwing expert *(yep, they exist)* before being let free to unleash your inner lumberjack. Top tip: make sure to wear a loose-fitting top and closed-toe shoes.

Sale Water Park
Sale Water Park, Rifle Rd, Sale M33 2LX

A 30-min journey outside of the city on the MetroLink takes you to this outdoor playground perfect for adventurous couples. During the warmer months, you can rent paddle boards, kayaks & canoes to explore the water. For those who prefer the safety of land, hire a bike or simply enjoy a scenic walk together.

Budget-friendly finds...

Northern Quarter
Northern Quarter, M4 1HQ

As Manchester's creative hub, the Northern Quarter is home to countless independent fashion stores, record shops, eateries and bars. For a fun date idea, why not spend an afternoon visiting the many vintage clothes shops and pick out outfits for each other to wear that evening!

Chinatown
Faulkner Street, M1 4FH

The third largest in the whole of Europe, Manchester's Chinatown is a splash of colour and flavour right in the city centre. Looking for some authentic Chinese, Thai or Japanese dishes? You'll both be spoilt for choice here. If visiting in January or February, make sure to attend the magical Chinese New Year festival!

Our visit to Manchester...

We visited...

☐ The Lowry

☐ HOME (Manchester)

☐ John Rylands Library

☐ Sale Water Park

☐ Chinatown

☐ ....

☐ ....

☐ Frog & Bucket Comedy Club

☐ Science & Industry Museum

☐ Whistle Punks Urban Axe Throwing

☐ Northern Quarter

☐ ....

☐ ....

☐ ....

Notes...

....

....

....

....

....

....

Rating: ♡♡♡♡♡

*Our favourite photo
from the weekend*

Date:

Location:

Caption:

Liverpool

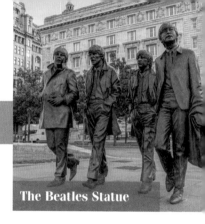

Best For: Amazing nightlife,
The Beatles, museums & history.

A fabulous city with rich history, Liverpool boasts an incredible nightlife and amazing music scene. Talking of which, Liverpool is packed with 'all night' clubs, cosy cocktail bars and live music venues to keep you both entertained until the early hours. It was named 'European Capital of Culture' in 2008 and has continued to thrive ever since. With an endless number of museums, galleries and unique attractions, Liverpool is one of the UK's best go-to couples weekend away destinations.

The Beatles Statue

Romance ♥♥♥♡♡
Food & Drink ♥♥♥♥♡
Things To See ♥♥♥♥♡
Natural Beauty ♥♥♡♡♡

River Mersey

Drive Time to Liverpool
From London | 4 hours
From Manchester | 1 hour
From Newcastle | 3 hours
From Birmingham | 2 hours
From Cardiff | 4 hours

Train Duration to Liverpool
From London | 2.5 hours
From Manchester | 1 hour
From Newcastle | 3 hours
From Birmingham | 2 hours
From Cardiff | 5.5 hours

Best Time to Visit...
There is a fair chance of rain all year round, with the summer months your best chance at avoiding the wet weather. From August to May is football season and hotels will be busier.

Best Places to Eat & Drink...

Duke St Food & Drink Market | Chic food hall with 6 eateries
46 Duke St, Liverpool L1 5AS

Amalia | Modern Italian food
2 Campbell Square, Liverpool L1 5FB

Smoke & Dough | Grill your meat at your table - unique & lively!
14 Paradise St, Liverpool L1 8JF

The Art School Restaurant | Fine dining (**live music on Saturday**)
1 Sugnall St, Liverpool L7 7EB

The Cavern Club | Live music; Birthplace of the Beatles!
10 Mathew St, Liverpool L2 6RE

Top Tip: Keep your bad attempt at the Liverpudlian accent (known locally as 'scouse') to yourselves, its considered to be quite rude and will probably be met with an eye roll or two.

The Royal Albert Dock

Accommodation

Novotel Liverpool Centre | 0151 702 5100
Merseyside, 40 Hanover St, Liverpool L1 4LN

The Resident Liverpool | 0151 705 2626
29 Seel St, Liverpool L1 4AU

Quest Liverpool Aparthotel | 0151 318 1809
72 Church St, Liverpool L1 3AY

The Municipal Hotel Liverpool | 0151 332 3030
Municipal Building, Dale St, Liverpool L2 2DH

Staybridge Suites Liverpool | 0151 703 9700
21 Keel Wharf, Liverpool L3 4FN

Pullman Liverpool | 0151 945 1000
King's Dock, Port of Liverpool, Liverpool L3 4FP

Titanic Hotel Liverpool | 0151 559 1444
Stanley Dock, Regent Rd, Liverpool L3 0AN

Radisson RED Hotel | 0151 212 3456
7 Lime St, Liverpool L1 1RD

All Bar One by Innkeepers Collection | 0151 227 3357
Derby Square, Liverpool L2 7NU

A Weekend Itinerary...

Day	Morning	Afternoon	Evening
Friday	Arrive in Liverpool	Explore the Royal Albert Dock	Enjoy the 'Alcotraz' experience or a Hope St Shivers ghost walk
Saturday	Visit the Beatles Story Museum or the Merseyside Maritime Museum	Fill your stomachs at Duke Street Food & Drink Market	Catch a show at Laughterhouse Comedy Club
Sunday	Relax at the Titanic Spa or take a cruise with Mersey Ferries	Wander around Sefton Park	Travel home

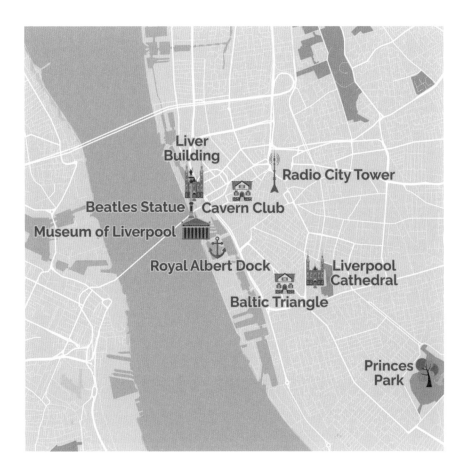

Best way to explore Liverpool...

Liverpool's main attractions are closely packed together which makes getting around on foot simple! There is also the 'Merseyrail' metro system and the Plusbus so you can reach all of Liverpool's attractions easily. For the more adventurous, bike hire is abundant and there are plenty of cycle route maps available.

 Did you know?

Liverpool is home to Europe's oldest Chinatown. You'll find it just off Duke Street, it's jam-packed with restaurants and supermarkets where you can enjoy authentic Chinese cuisine.

Top picks for slowing down...

Titanic Hotel Underground Spa
22 Regent Rd, L3 0AN

Underneath the Titanic Hotel sits the Maya Blue Wellness Spa. Between red brick arches you'll find hydrotherapy pools, foot baths, a health & fitness centre and a tea garden – the spa offers a unique place to unwind. You can have 2 hours access to the thermal site or buy a package and combine with a treatment.

Laughterhouse Comedy Club
13-15 Fenwick St, L2 7LS

If you fancy doing something a little less active but still just as fun, head to Liverpool's best comedy club. The intimate setting creates a great atmosphere for a comedy night! Each show has three comedians, a compere and of course a bar. Everything you need for a laughter-filled date night in Liverpool!

Unique things to see & do...

The Beatles Story Museum
Britannia Vaults, Royal Albert Dock, L3 4AD

You'll be taken on an immersive journey through the lives of The Beatles. A must-do on your trip to Liverpool! There's amazing replicas of Abbey Road Studios and The Cavern so you'll feel as though you're in the 60s, experiencing the places that made The Beatles so famous.

The Royal Albert Dock
L3 4AD

The most-visited tourist destination in Liverpool, home to amazing museums, galleries, restaurants, bars and shops. There's so much to do here you could spend hours exploring. Why not try an escape room together? Or visit the International Slavery Museum and learn about Liverpool's dark history.

Mersey Maritime Museum

Sefton Park

The Royal Albert Dock

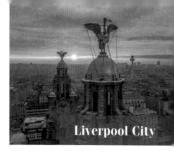
Liverpool City

Top picks for adventure seekers...

Mersey Ferries Explorer Cruise
Pier Head, George Parade, L3 1DP

The ultimate way to see the top sights of Liverpool and learn about the fascinating history of the River Mersey. You can even take a boat ride all the way to Manchester from here! But the most popular cruise is the 50-minute river explorer cruises and from only £12 per person, it's great value for money!

Hope St Shivers
Start Location; Outside The Philharmonic Pub, Hope Street, City Centre

Liverpool's most famous historic ghost walk, this eerie 1.5 hour guided walk will take you through the Cathedral Quarter, you'll visit two incredible cathedrals and walk down the "most haunted Street in Northern England". This one's not for the faint hearted - spooky, yet informative and fun!

Alcotraz
36 Seel Street, L1 4BE

Looking for something different? Enjoy this theatrical experience as you sit inside a 'cell-block' dressed in orange overalls and watch the live actors act out the storyline. You'll need to 'smuggle' your alcohol into the prison and the bartender 'inmates' will provide everything else & make you some bespoke cocktails.

Budget-friendly finds...

Sefton Park
Aigburth, Merseyside L17 1AP

A lush, green, 200-acre park located towards the south of the city. In the centre of the park you'll find the stunning glass Victorian Palm House (home to an array of botanical plants). Near the boating lake you can explore caves, waterfalls and you can also rent bikes to further discover the magic of Sefton Park.

Mersey Maritime Museum
Royal Albert Dock, L3 4AQ

Completely free to visit and perfect for curious couples! The maritime museum explores Liverpool's past including the slave trade, titanic and life at sea. There are various exhibitions added throughout the year, some may require an admission fee. Visit the website to find out what's on before you visit.

Our visit to Liverpool...

We visited...

☐ The Royal Albert Dock

☐ Hope St Shivers

☐ Mersey Ferries Explorer Cruise

☐ Mersey Maritime Museum

☐ Alcotraz

☐ ....

☐ ....

☐ The Beatles Story Museum

☐ Laughterhouse Comedy Club

☐ Sefton Park

☐ Titanic Hotel Underground Spa

☐ ....

☐ ....

☐ ....

Notes...

....

....

....

....

....

....

Rating: ♡♡♡♡♡

*Our favourite photo
from the weekend*

Date:

Location:

Caption:

Chester

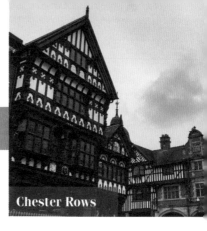

A unique, charming and historic city which makes for a perfect couples escape. Chester is a compact city complete with a thriving food scene, superb nightlife and all kinds of adventures to be had. Wander around the city walls, take a tour of Chester Cathedral, head for an adrenaline filled white water kayaking experience or visit Chester's epic zoo! There's just about something for everyone in this unique Northwest city.

Chester Rows

Romance ❤❤❤❤♡
Food & Drink ❤❤❤❤♡
Things To See ❤❤❤❤♡
Natural Beauty ❤❤♡♡♡

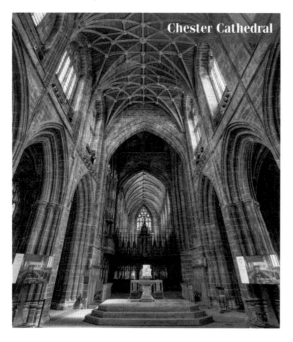

Chester Cathedral

Drive Time to Chester
From London | 4 hours
From Manchester | 1 hour
From Newcastle | 3.5 hours
From Birmingham | 2 hours
From Cardiff | 4 hours

Train Duration to Chester
From London | 3 hours
From Manchester | 1.5 hours
From Newcastle | 4.5 hours
From Birmingham | 2 hours
From Cardiff | 3 hours

Best Time to Visit...
Spring & Summer - Both seasons host an array of festivals and events that see the city come alive, such as the Boodles May Festival at Chester Racecourse *(in May)*, Chester7s Sport & Music Festival *(in June)* and Chester's Heritage Festival *(in June)*.
Winter - A magical time to visit the city and its Christmas Market in November and December.

Best Places to Eat & Drink...

Hanky Panky | Pancake heaven
20 Commonhall Street, Chester CH1 2BJ

The Old Harkers Arms | Good pub grub
1 Russell Street, Chester CH3 5AL

Da Noi | Fine Italian cuisine
63 Bridge Street, Chester CH1 1NG

Siam Thai & Teppanyaki Restaurant | Family run Asian eatery
32 City Road, Chester CH1 3AE

The Love Shack | Tiki bar offering cocktails, food and music
14 Cuppin Street, Chester CH1 2BN

Top Tip: Head to Chester's cross junction, where the city's four main streets come together, to soak in the atmosphere and watch buskers perform.

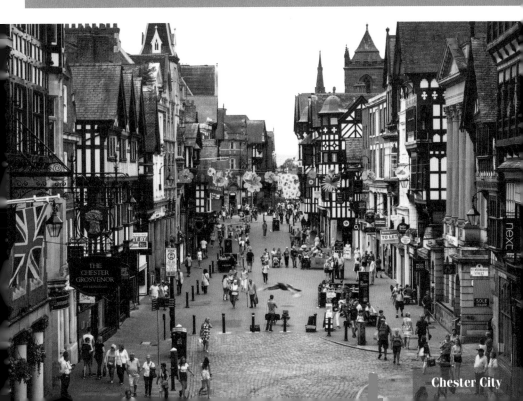

Chester City

Accommodation

£

Moxy Chester | 0124 464 6002
71 Boughton, Chester CH3 5BS

ABode Chester | 0124 434 7000
Grosvenor Road, Chester CH1 2DJ

MILL Hotel & Spa | 0124 435 0035
Milton Street, Chester CH1 3NF

££

Hotel Indigo Chester | 0124 473 5745
Grosvenor Park Road, Chester CH1 1QQ

The Boathouse Inn & Riverside Rooms | 0124 432 8709
21 The Groves, Chester CH1 1SD

Oddfellows Chester | 0124 4345 454
20 Lower Bridge St, Chester CH1 1RS

£££

Stone Villa Chester | 0124 434 5014
3 Stone Place, Chester CH2 3NR

The Chester Grosvenor | 0124 432 4024
Eastgate, Chester CH1 1LT

Bridge Street Apartments | 0124 488 8815
14a Bridge St, Chester CH1 1NN

A Weekend Itinerary...

Day	Morning	Afternoon	Evening
Friday	Arrive in Chester	Take a stroll along Chester City Walls	Catch a show at the Storyhouse
Saturday	Explore Chester Cathedral	Enjoy a cruise along the River Dee	Dinner and drinks at the Love Shack
Sunday	Visit the Sick to Death attraction	Wander around Chester Rows	Travel home

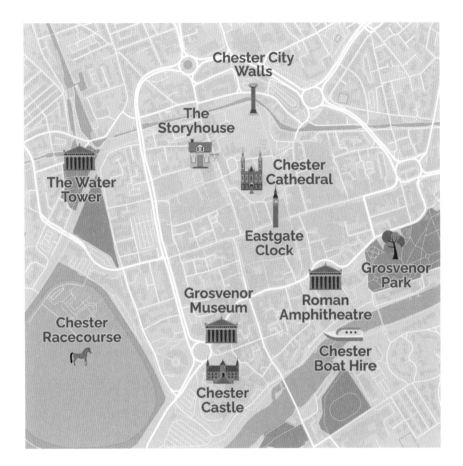

Best way to explore Chester...

Chester is a compact city that's easily walkable. The hop-on hop-off bus is a solid option if you'd prefer a more relaxing way to see all of the sights. If you're heading for Chester Zoo, you'll need to drive or catch a bus as its located 3.5 miles outside of the city centre *(definitely worth the journey though)*.

(i) **Did you know?**

Chester Racecourse was once a harbour. Established back in 1539, it is renowned as the oldest active race-course in the world. However, most of its current 65-acre site was not always dry land; in fact, it was an important river harbour on the Dee.

Top picks for slowing down...

River Cruises
Souter's Lane, The Groves, CH1 1SZ

Take a relaxing ride along the River Dee on either a half an hour or two hour tour. Save money by pre-booking online, you could even buy a combined boat and sightseeing bus ticket. For an even more romantic experience, book a private picnic boat tour *(although it's quite pricey!)*.

The Storyhouse
Hunter Street, CH1 2AR

Sit back and enjoy a live show or a film at 'Chester's cultural centre'. The venue houses an 800-seat auditorium, a 150-seat theatre, an independent cinema and a library – as well as a restaurant and bar. In the summer they host an open-air theatre at the nearby Grosvenor Park so look out for tickets if you're visiting in July or August.

Unique things to see & do...

Chester City Walls
Vicar's Lane, CH1 1QX

Visit the oldest, longest and most complete city walls in Britain. An ideal way to see the city, the full circuit spans around 2 miles and will take about 40 minutes to walk. If you don't fancy the whole walk there are four main gateways you can enter and exit the route from. Spot the Roman Amphitheatre along the way!

Chester Zoo
Upton-by-Chester, CH2 1EU

Are you both animal lovers? Visit the epic 128-acre Chester Zoo, home to over 21,000 animals! Make sure you enjoy a lazy river boat ride on the unique 'island' *(purple on the map)*. Is it a special occasion? You could book an animal experience for an up-close interaction. Pre-book tickets online.

Sick to Death
St Michael's Church, Bridge Street, CH1 1NW

This is certainly a unique, weird and wonderful attraction! Located in a Grade II listed church on the Medieval Rows. Take a self-guided tour and learn about medicine through time. You'll experience some odd smells, interactive displays *(such as the autopsy room)* and intriguing artefacts *(such as a plague doctors mask)*.

Chester City Walls

Chester Zoo

Chester Cathedral

Chester Rows

Top picks for adventure seekers...

Chester Cycle Hire
Victoria Lodge Guest House, 64 Hoole Road, CH2 3NL

Explore the city on two wheels! Hire a bike and head out on one of the many cycle paths around the city and along the Canalside. If you fancy a more leisurely ride then hire a tandem bicycle and sit on the back! Helmets, locks, maps and puncture repair kits are all provided at no extra cost.

Dee River Kayaking
Sandy Lane Park, CH3 5UL

If you're looking for adventure then head for a kayaking experience! You can choose from white water kayaking *(for adrenaline junkies)*, a more peaceful kayaking experience or even a paddleboarding session on calmer waters. Pre-book online. There are no changing facilities so bring a changing robe for modesty!

Budget-friendly finds...

Countess of Chester Country Park
Valley Drive, CH2 1UL

A peaceful park, that's located adjacent to the city's hospital. Take a relaxing stroll around the park's pathways and explore the surrounding woodland, wetland and meadowland that's inhabited by an array of wildlife such as the Kingfisher, Greater Spotted Woodpecker and many species of Butterfly.

Chester Rows
Bridge St, Watergate St, Eastgate St & Northgate St, CH1 1NG

These two-tiered timber-framed galleries line the main streets of the city, forming a second row of shops above street level. They date back as far as the 13th century and historically this is where the city's residents would come to trade, dine and drink. Today, The Rows are home to independent shops, bars & restaurants so head for a wander!

Chester Cathedral
St Werburgh Street, CH1 2DY

The impressive architecture here is reason to visit alone. Entry is free; however, there are several tours you could book onto for a fee, including the tower tour – where you'll climb 216 steps for incredible views! Treat yourselves to an afternoon tea in the café *(set inside the 13th century monks dining hall)*.

Our visit to Chester...

We visited...

☐ River Cruises

☐ Chester City Walls

☐ Sick to Death

☐ Chester Cycle Hire

☐ Chester Rows

☐ ....

☐ ....

☐ The Storyhouse

☐ Chester Zoo

☐ Countess of Chester County Park

☐ Dee River Kayaking

☐ Chester Cathedral

☐ ....

☐ ....

Notes...

....

....

....

....

....

....

Rating: ♡♡♡♡♡

*Our favourite photo
from the weekend*

Date:

Location:

Caption:

Yorkshire &
The Humber

Yorkshire Dales

Home to some of the UK's most breath-taking landscapes, picturesque villages and historic significance, the Yorkshire Dales National Park is the ideal destination for couples who love the outdoors and want to escape the hustle and bustle. Spend your days hiking the region's endless trails before cosying up together at one of the many welcoming pubs – think fireplaces, cute dogs and good hearty food! Whether you both want to chill and unwind or get your heart pumping, the Yorkshire Dales has it all.

Ribblehead Viaduct

Romance ♥♥♥♥♡
Food & Drink ♥♥♥♡♡
Things To See ♥♥♥♥♡
Natural Beauty ♥♥♥♥♥

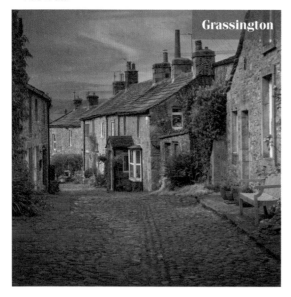

Grassington

Drive Time to Yorkshire
From London | 5.5 hours
From Manchester | 2.5 hours
From Newcastle | 2 hours
From Birmingham | 3.5 hours
From Cardiff | 5.5 hours

Train Duration to Yorkshire
From London | 5 hours
From Manchester | 3.5 hours
From Newcastle | 3 hours
From Birmingham | 4.5 hours
From Cardiff | 7 hours

Best Time to Visit...
Summer- If you're both looking for plenty of sunshine, some warmth and lots of daylight, May through to August is the best time to explore the Yorkshire Dales.
Autumn - The weather will be less predictable but it can be well worth the risk to take in this beautiful region after summer, as the landscape transforms into an autumnal paradise of reds, oranges and yellows!

Best Places to Eat & Drink...

Laburnum House Hawes Tea Room | Locally sourced treats
Laburnum House The Holme, Hawes DL8 3QR

The Queens Arms Restaurant | Comforting Yorkshire pub
Litton BD23 5QJ

The Angel Inn Restaurant | Michelin star in a traditional pub setting
Main St, Hetton BD23 6LT

The Secret Garden | Plant-based restaurant overlooking a river
Cove Road Beck Hall Hotel, Malham BD23 4DJ

The OPO Bar | A super friendly bar with live music
8 High Street, Ingleton LA6 3AA

Top Tip: The Yorkshire Dales is home to some of the darkest skies in the country and has four dark sky discovery sites, so make sure to add stargazing to your itinerary!

Yorkshire Dales

Accommodation

£

Grassington Lodge | 0175 675 2518
8 Wood Lane, Grassington BD23 5LU

Kings Arms Hotel | 0174 888 4259
High Lane, Reeth DL11 6SY

Ashfield House | 0175 675 2584
3 Summers Fold, Grassington BD23 5AE

££

Green Grove Country House | 0172 9830 526
Bell Busk, BD23 4DU

The Traddock | 0152 425 1224
Austwick, Settle LA2 8BY

Black Horse Hotel | 0175 675 2770
4 Garrs Lane, Grassington BD23 5AT

£££

Yorebridge House | 0196 965 2060
Yorebridge House, Bainbridge DL8 3EE

The Devonshire Arms Hotel & Spa | 0175 671 8100
Bolton Abbey Estate, Yorkshire Dales National Park BD23 6AJ

The Burgoyne Hotel | 0174 888 4292
On The Green, Reeth DL11 6SN

A Weekend Itinerary...

Day	Morning	Afternoon	Evening
Friday	Arrive in the Yorkshire Dales	Explore Ribblehead Viaduct	Drinks at The OPO Bar
Saturday	Explore Malham Cove, Gordale Scar & Janet's Foss	Visit Grassington village	Devonshire Spa Twilight Session
Sunday	Enjoy some cheese at Wensleydale Creamery	Explore Bolton Castle	Travel home

Best way to explore the Yorkshire Dales...

It's best to travel by car when heading to the Yorkshire Dales. Unlike many city breaks, local transport options will be minimal and with four wheels you can explore more of the 841 square miles of stunning landscape on offer! If you're into cycling, some of the UK's best cycling roads are found across Yorkshire!

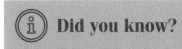 **Did you know?**

The Yorkshire Dales are home to the famous Wensleydale cheese, so keep your eyes peeled for Wallace and Gromit! The region also has its own 'Three Peaks Challenge', where hikers climb to the top of Pen-y-ghent, Whernside and Ingleborough all in 12 hours or under.

Top picks for slowing down...

Devonshire Spa
Bolton Bridge, Skipton
BD23 6AJ

After exploring the Yorkshire Dales on foot, sooth your muscles in a luxurious, relaxing spa. Enjoy a treatment together before hopping from saunas to steam rooms to jacuzzis. There are several spas within the area; however, Devonshire Spa offers a wide variety of packages and is highly rated by reviewers!

Grassington
The Square, Grassington,
Skipton BD23 5AQ

Spend a relaxing afternoon wandering around the picturesque village of Grassington together *(you might recognise Grassington as the historic village that's featured in the TV series 'All Creatures Great and Small')*. Enjoy a cuppa and sweet treat from Love Brownies or grab a pint at The Devonshire pub.

Unique things to see & do...

Wensleydale Creamery
Gayle Lane, Wensleydale,
Hawes DL8 3RN

For cheese lovers, a visit to Wensleydale Creamery is an absolute must *(more cheese Gromit!)*. Not only can you enjoy some of the finest Wensleydale cheese available, you can join their award-winning 'Cheese Experience'. Watch as experts carefully craft the cheese by hand and offer plenty of wisdom on the art of cheesemaking!

Malham Cove, Gordale Scar & Janet's Foss
Malham, Skipton BD23 4DA

Just a short walk from Malham village leads you to the start of a 5-mile walk covering the natural beauty of Malham's surrounding area. The circular trail will take you and your partner to Janet's Foss, a beautiful waterfall, the 100m-high cliffs of Gordale Scar and finally the famous limestone pavement above Malham Cove.

Bolton Castle
Nr Leyburn,
DL8 4ET

Step back in time and spend a day exploring over 600 years of Yorkshire history at Bolton Castle. From re-enactments to falconry displays to a magnificent-looking tearoom, you could both easily spend hours taking in all the sights of this castle! Please note the castle is open from March to November each year.

Forbidden Corner
Tupgill Park Estate,
Middleham, Leyburn DL8 4TJ

A quirky attraction for young at heart couples! Explore the incredibly scenic four-acre garden that's filled with a labyrinth of tunnels, chambers, pathways and surprises; including a translucent glass pyramid, various mazes, stepping stones and 'traps' that spray water – so watch out! Pre-booking is essential.

Aysgarth Falls

Malham Cove

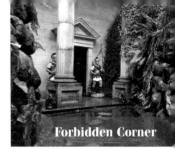
Forbidden Corner

Top picks for adventure seekers...

White Scar Cave
Carnforth, LA6 3AW

The longest show cave in Britain, White Scar Cave is a fascinating natural attraction. Join a guided tour which takes you through the 1-mile underground tunnel, exploring all its hidden wonders. Weather conditions can impact accessibility, so make sure to check the official White Scar Cave website before visiting.

Climbing & Abseiling
Hornby Laithe, Stainforth, Settle BD24 9PB

The Yorkshire Dales' limestone crags are ideal for thrill seekers looking to strap in and spend some time climbing or abseiling. The Yorkshire Dales Guides offer plenty of experiences led by specialists – for beginners up to experts. You'll both be supplied with all the equipment, just bring yourselves *(and some courage!)*.

Mountain Biking
Various Locations

Feel the wind in your hair and the adrenaline coursing through your veins as you both take on the many mountain bike trails the Yorkshire Dales has to offer. With a network of over 560 miles of bridleways, byways and green lanes, it's a great destination for all levels. Pack your own bikes or hire locally!

Budget-friendly finds...

Ribblehead Viaduct
Low Sleights Road, Carnforth LA6 3AU

Perfect for photographers or for taking an atmospheric, romantic walk together, the Ribblehead Viaduct is a beautiful Grade II listed structure. It carries the Settle–Carlisle railway over the Batty Moss and was built all the way back in 1875. Get up close to the viaduct and you may even catch a steam engine crossover!

Aysgarth Falls
Aysgarth Falls National Park Centre, Church Bank, Aysgarth, Leyburn DL8 3TH

Accessible via a short climb from the car park these three stepped waterfalls are a thing of beauty! Situated on the River Ure, the falls are surrounded by woodland and farmland – they were even featured in a scene for the film 'Robin Hood Prince of Thieves'. Access to the falls is free; however, there is a small fee to park at the visitor centre.

Our visit to the Yorkshire Dales...

Date visited:

We visited...

- [ ] Devonshire Spa
- [ ] Wensleydale Creamery
- [ ] Forbidden Corner
- [ ] White Scar Cave
- [ ] Aysgarth Falls
- [ ] ....
- [ ] ....

- [ ] Grassington
- [ ] Bolton Castle
- [ ] Malham Cove, Gordale Scar & Janet's Foss
- [ ] Ribblehead Viaduct
- [ ] ....
- [ ] ....
- [ ] ....

Notes...

....

....

....

....

....

....

Rating: ♡ ♡ ♡ ♡ ♡

*Our favourite photo
from the weekend*

Date:

Location:

Caption:

York

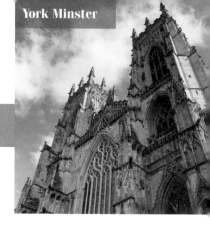
York Minster

A vibrant city with Roman roots and a Viking past, offering an epic couples weekend away. From the buzzing streets of The Shambles *(which inspired Diagon Alley from Harry Potter)* to the historic city walls, to the thriving foodie scene. Visit the iconic Betty's Café Tea Rooms for an afternoon treat or York's Chocolate Story to unwrap the history of chocolate. The compact city of York is easy to cover on foot and has an awful lot to offer. This is without a doubt, one of the best UK getaways, we're positive you'll absolutely love it...

Romance ♥♥♥♥♡
Food & Drink ♥♥♥♥♥
Things To See ♥♥♥♥♥
Natural Beauty ♥♥♥♡♡

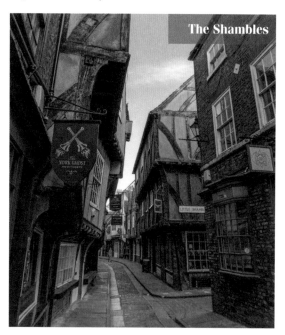
The Shambles

Drive Time to York
From London | 4 hours
From Manchester | 2 hours
From Newcastle | 2 hours
From Birmingham | 3 hours
From Cardiff | 5 hours

Train Duration to York
From London | 4 hours
From Manchester | 3 hours
From Newcastle | 2 hours
From Birmingham | 3 hours
From Cardiff | 5 hours

Best Time to Visit...
Spring - Visit in March or April for less crowds but a chance of decent weather.
Winter - The Christmas Market in December offers a unique opportunity to explore York's iconic festive markets.

Best Places to Eat & Drink...

Betty's Café Tea Rooms | Luxury afternoon tea
6-8 St. Helen's Square, York YO1 8QP

Partisan | Independent restaurant, café & arts space
112 Micklegate, York YO1 6JX

Mannion & Co | Bistro breakfast & lunch
1 Blake Street, York YO1 8QJ

Melton's | Fabulous fine dining
7 Scarcroft Road, York YO23 1ND

Kings Arms | Pub on the River Ouse
3 King's Staith, York YO1 9SN

Top Tip: Purchase a York Pass to save money across multiple attractions including JORVIK Viking Centre, York Minster, the National Railway Museum and Clifford's Tower.

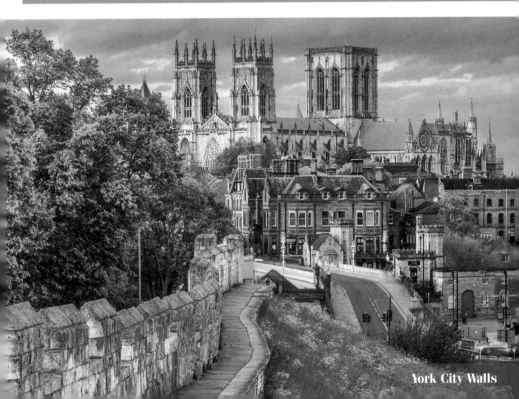

York City Walls

Accommodation

£

Premier Inn York City | 0333 321 9197
Blossom Street, York YO24 1AJ

Clementines Town House Hotel | 0190 464 0101
4-5 St Peter's Grove, Clifton, York YO30 6AQ

B+B York | 0190 455 9777
15 St Peter's Grove, Clifton, York YO30 6AQ

££

Roomzzz York City | 0190 480 9888
Terry Avenue, York, YO23 1FG

No.1 By GuestHouse | 0190 464 4744
1 Clifton, York YO30 6AA

The Fat Badger | 0190 461 2078
2-4 High Petergate, York YO1 7EH

£££

The Grand | 0190 438 0038
Station Rise, York YO1 6GD

Middlethorpe Hall & Spa | 0190 464 1241
Bishopthorpe Road, York YO23 2GB

Judges Court House | 0190 467 6184
Coney Street, York YO1 9ND

A Weekend Itinerary...

Day	Morning	Afternoon	Evening
Friday	Arrive in York	Clifford's Tower & JORVIK Viking Centre	The Ghost Bus Tour
Saturday	River Ouse Cruise	Afternoon Tea at Betty's	The York Dungeon
Sunday	The Shambles	York City Walls Walking Trail	Travel home

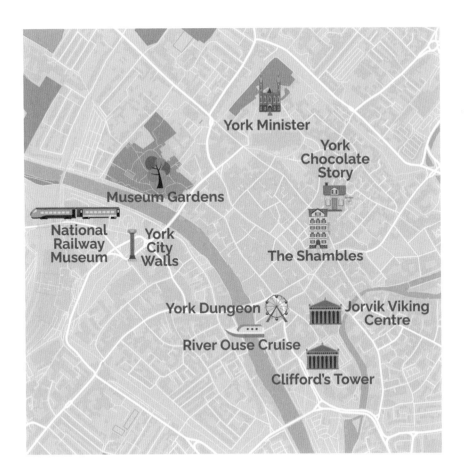

Best way to explore York...

York is a compact city that's best explored on foot. Adventurous couples may opt to hire a bike or an e-scooter for a quicker way to explore the city. Don't forget the River Ouse boat cruises, you can even hire your own self-drive boat for a different perspective.

 Did you know?

There are over 20 cat statues hidden randomly all over the city centre. You could follow the Lucky Cat Trail and see if you can spot them (you may have to look up to find some).

Top picks for slowing down...

River Ouse Cruise
Kings Staith, YO1 9SN

Offering a relaxing way to see the city from a new perspective, whilst learning all about York's history from the on-board tour guide. The cruise lasts for around 45 minutes and you must pre-book, a free trip can be redeemed if you buy a York Pass, although its good value for money anyway!

Unique things to see & do...

The Ghost Bus Tours York
Station Rd, Bus stop RE, YO24 1AA

Spend an evening enjoying this comedy-horror theatrical tour on wheels. Lasting around 60-75 minutes, you'll encounter York's top attractions and learn about the city's haunted history. If you fancy something a little less 'gimmicky' and a bit more serious, then try a ghost walking tour.

York Minister
Deangate, YO1 7HH

A gothic cathedral of epic proportions! Explore this sacred space, climb the Central towers 275 steps for panoramic views of the city or take the Hidden Minster Tour to discover spaces normally closed to the public. Tickers are valid for a year, take one of the free guided tours to get the most out of your visit.

JORVIK Viking Centre
19 Coppergate, YO1 9WT

One for history lovers, this unique attraction gives you a snapshot of what Viking life would have been like as you take a tram ride through the reconstructed city of Jorvik (complete with realistic sounds and smells from the Viking Age). You'll then have chance to look through the collection of artefacts in the gallery area.

York's Chocolate Story
King's Square, YO1 7LD

A must-do for chocolate lovers! Where you'll 'unwrap the history of chocolate', as well as how it's made and *(the best bit)*, how to taste like an expert! If you book online in advance, you can save 10% on standard tours. Allow around 90-minutes to complete the tour. Head to the café and shop afterwards for more sweet treats!

River Ouse

Clifford's Tower

National Railway Museum

Top picks for adventure seekers...

The York Dungeon
12 Clifford St, YO1 9RD

Not for the easily spooked, this thrilling attraction combines story-telling, horror and humour. You'll be guided through immersive sets as live actors take you back in time through York's darkest history – see, hear and smell the cities murky past! The tour lasts for an hour and pre-booking is essential.

Clifford's Tower
Tower Street, YO1 9SA

The largest remaining building of York Castle, Clifford's Tower is set upon a mound and offers 360-degree views over the city from the towers roof deck. You can also explore inside the tower via the internal walkways. Book online or pay on arrival, its free to enter for English Heritage members.

Budget-friendly finds...

The Shambles
Shambles, YO1 7LZ

The renowned cobbled street with overhanging buildings that's believed to have been the inspiration for Diagon Alley in the Harry Potter film series. The Shambles dates back to medieval times and was once full of butcher shops. Today its filled with mostly independent retailers and cafés.

National Railway Museum
Leeman Road, YO26 4XJ

Train enthusiast or not, this museum is impressive. View the huge collection of trains from past and present innovation and learn the story of rail transport in Britain. Enjoy the flying Scotsman VR experience and more. Its free entry, although donations are very much welcomed!

York City Walls
YO1 7LJ

Take a walk around York's City Walls that stretch around the city for 3.4km *(about 2 miles)*. The full route will take you around 2 hours – they are the longest medieval town walls in England after all! The walking trail is free to access, and you can grab an online guide at yorkwalls.org.uk.

Our visit to York...

We visited...

☐ York Minister

☐ The Shambles

☐ York City Walls

☐ The York Dungeon

☐ JORVIK Viking Centre

☐ ....

☐ ....

☐ River Ouse Cruise

☐ Clifford's Tower

☐ National Railway Museum

☐ The Ghost Bus Tours York

☐ York's Chocolate Story

☐ ....

☐ ....

Notes...

....

....

....

....

....

....

Rating: ♡♡♡♡♡

*Our favourite photo
from the weekend*

Date:

Location:

Caption:

Leeds

Leeds Street Art Trail

Known for its independent nature, culinary delights and affordable prices, Leeds is a great destination for a weekend away with your partner. Spend the daytime exploring the city's galleries and shops while topping up on coffee before dressing up for a night on the town. For those looking to live a little slower, catch a show at the theatre and enjoy some feline cuddling at a cat café. Whatever your choice, Leeds offers an unforgettable couples' weekend!

Romance ♥♥♥♥♡
Food & Drink ♥♥♥♥♡
Things To See ♥♥♥♡♡
Natural Beauty ♥♥♥♡♡

Leeds City

Drive Time to Leeds
From London | 4 hours
From Manchester | 1.5 hours
From Newcastle | 2 hours
From Birmingham | 2.5 hours
From Cardiff | 4.5 hours

Train Duration to Leeds
From London | 2.5 hours
From Manchester | 1 hour
From Newcastle | 2 hours
From Birmingham | 2 hours
From Cardiff | 4 hours

Best Time to Visit...
Summer - The warmer months are a great time to explore Leeds, thanks to the more comfortable climate *(especially if you're not used to Yorkshire weather!)* and never getting quite as crowded as other major UK cities.
Winter - The weather might be a little colder, but winter is a great, even more affordable time to visit Leeds, where you can also enjoy the city's beautiful Christmas market.

Best Places to Eat & Drink...

Olive & Rye | Independent café perfect for breakfast
18-20 Queens Arcade Briggate, Leeds LS1 6LF

La Taberna Leeds | Atmospheric romantic restaurant
Britannia House 16 York Place Basement Britannia House, Leeds LS1 2EU

The Dry Dock Leeds | A bar on a boat!
Woodhouse Lane, Leeds LS2 3AX

Chef Jono at V&V | Flavourful fine dining
68 New Briggate, Leeds LS1 6NU

La Piola Italian Delicatessen | A tasty slice of Italy in Leeds
2 Park Square East, Leeds LS1 2NE

> **Top Tip:** Look out for the incredible artwork dotted around the city on buildings, walkways, walls and even boats, all part of Leeds 'Street Art Trail'. Find locations for the artwork online.

Leeds City

Accommodation

£

easyHotel Leeds City Centre | 0113 531 0505
18-22 Lands Lane, Leeds LS1 6LB

Roomzzz Aparthotel Leeds City West | 0113 233 0400
2 Burley Rd, Woodhouse, Leeds LS3 1JB

Premier Inn Leeds City Centre | 0333 234 6551
1 Whitehall Quay, Riverside, Lower Wortley, Leeds LS1 4EQ

££

Malmaison Leeds | 0113 426 0047
1 Swinegate, Leeds LS1 4AG

Clayton Hotel Leeds | 0113 234 2340
Sweet St, Holbeck, Leeds LS11 9AT

Leeds Marriott Hotel | 0113 236 6366
4 Trevelyan Square Boar Lane, Leeds LS1 6ET

£££

The Chambers Park Place | 0113 386 3300
30 Park Place, Leeds LS1 2SP

The Queens Hotel | 0113 243 1323
City Square, Leeds LS1 1PJ

Dakota Leeds | 0113 322 6261
8 Russell Street, Leeds LS1 5RN

A Weekend Itinerary...

Day	Morning	Afternoon	Evening
Friday	Arrive in Leeds	Get competitive at Arcade Club Leeds	Take a cocktail master-class at Liquor Studio
Saturday	Shop independents at Leeds Corn Exchange	Visit the Kitty Café (if you're cat lovers!)	Enjoy comedy at the HiFi Club
Sunday	Grab some breakfast at Olive & Rye	Explore Leeds Art Gallery	Travel home

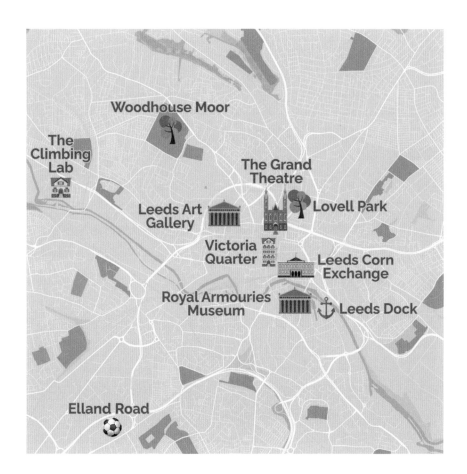

Best way to explore Leeds..

Despite its popularity and cultural significance, Leeds' city centre is quite compact and easily explored on foot. If you're heading outside of the city, hop aboard the LeedsCityBus for a very affordable journey. Enjoy travelling on two wheels? Hire a bike for the day!

(ⓘ) Did you know?

Forget Hollywood, did you know the motion picture industry can actually trace its roots back to Leeds? Back in 1888 a Frenchman named Louis Le Prince recorded moving images for the first time in history at Oakwood Grange and Leeds Bridge.

Top picks for slowing down...

Comedy at the HiFi Club
2 Central Road, LS1 6DE

Every Saturday at the HiFi Club, the finest up-and-coming comedians take to the stage for an evening of belly-aching laughter. Previous comedy superstars to perform at the HiFi Club include Katherine Ryan, Alan Carr and John Bishop. Seating is allocated on a first come first serve basis so arrive early!

Leeds Grand Theatre
46 New Briggate, LS1 6NU

Leeds Grand Theatre, affectionately known as the *'Grand Old Lady of Leeds'* definitely lives up to its name. Blending both Romanesque and Gothic styles, the Grade II listed building is one of the most impressive theatres in the UK. Why not add more class to your visit and head to Bar 1878 for a pre-show beverage!

Unique things to see & do...

Kitty Café
8-9 Kirkgate, LS1 6BZ

The purrfect way to spend a Caturday afternoon? Sipping on a cappurrcino and cuddling a friendly feline – meow we're talking! If you didn't cringe at that, well done, but let's face it – spending an hour or two with your partner drinking coffee surrounded by cats does sound pretty relaxing!

Arcade Club
Abbey Retail Park, Savins Mill Way, Kirkstall, LS5 3RP

If you and your significant other have a competitive edge, you'll want to get down to Arcade Club. From old-school classics to modern games, plenty of entertainment is to be had. Although there are more central game-inspired bars in Leeds, Arcade Club is by far the largest and most affordable of them all!

Cocktail Masterclass at Liquor Studio
156a Lower Briggate, LS1 6LY

Fed up with beers, wines and ciders? Join a 'Cocktail Masterclass' at Liquor Studios and learn how to make delicious tipples from their award-winning team. You'll both create three bespoke cocktails during the 90-minute class. Make sure to book ahead of time and let the team know about any dietary requirements.

Leeds Street Art Trail

Leeds Corn Exchange

Leeds Dock

Top picks for adventure seekers...

Escape Room
Various locations

Is there a better way to bond and work together than during the manic madness of trying to escape from a locked room? We don't think so! You're spoilt for choice in Leeds, with a wide range of escape rooms on offer – from spooky, ghost-inspired rooms to WWII spy adventures! Pre-booking is essential with all companies.

The Climbing Lab
Kirkstall Industrial Park, 12, 14 & 15, LS4 2AZ

Pump a little adrenaline into your veins with a trip to Leeds' premium, cutting-edge indoor bouldering centre. With routes for beginners all the way up to 'ninjas', everyone is welcome. If you're both first-time climbers, you'll need to book an introductory session before taking to the walls by yourself.

Budget-friendly finds...

Leeds Corn Exchange
Call Lane, LS1 7BR

Housed inside a gorgeous Grade I listed building, Leeds Corn Exchange is home to some incredible independent shops and eateries. Self-confessed as a 'beacon of creativity shining against the mainstream' it's the ideal location to grab yourself some one-of-a-kind clothing and enjoy a non-corporate cup of coffee.

Leeds Art Gallery
The Headrow, LS1 3AA

Found in the heart of Leeds and free to visit, Leeds Art Gallery is a great spot to spend a few hours wandering exhibitions together. With a focus on British artists, the gallery includes acclaimed prints, watercolours, photography and contemporary art. Its beautiful café is also well worth a visit!

119

Our visit to Leeds...

We visited...

☐ The HiFi Club   ☐ Leeds Grand Theatre

☐ Kitty Café   ☐ Arcade Club

☐ The Liquor Studio   ☐ Escape Room

☐ The Climbing Lab   ☐ Leeds Corn Exchange

☐ Leeds Art Gallery   ☐ ....

☐ ....   ☐ ....

☐ ....   ☐ ....

Notes...

....

....

....

....

....

....

Rating: ♡♡♡♡♡

120

*Our favourite photo
from the weekend*

Date:

Location:

Caption:

Wales

Snowdonia
Otherwise known as Eryri

Wakin Path Waterfalls

The incredible Eryri National Park (better known as Snowdonia) is packed with rugged mountainous landscapes, spectacular waterfalls, hiking trails, quaint towns and epic castles. One for adrenaline junkies, hikers and outdoors loving couples alike, it's the ideal destination for an adventurous, wholesome weekend away! Why not climb the mighty mount Snowdon *(the highest mountain in Wales)* and then cosy up in a glamping pod under the stars.

Romance ♥♥♥♥♡
Food & Drink ♥♥♥♡♡
Things To See ♥♥♥♥♡
Natural Beauty ♥♥♥♥♥

Betws-y-Coed

Drive Time to Snowdonia
From London | 5 hours
From Manchester | 2 hours
From Newcastle | 4.5 hours
From Birmingham | 3 hours
From Cardiff | 3 hours

Train to Betws-y-Coed
From London | 4 hours
From Manchester | 3 hours
From Newcastle | 6 hours
From Birmingham | 4 hours
From Cardiff | 5 hours

Best Time to Visit...
Spring - You'll hopefully be able to reach mount Snowdon without a crowd at the summit *(always check the forecast before heading up!)*.
Winter - Hiking is not recommended during the winter season and the Snowdon Mountain Railway is closed; however, this could be a quieter time to enjoy places like Barmouth and Portmeiror.

Best Places to Eat & Drink...

Caffi Gwynant | Delicious breakfast & lunch **(near Mount Snowdon)**
Bethania, Nant Gwynant, Caernarfon LL55 4NL

Celtic Cabin | Tasty beach side wraps & quesadillas
The Promenade, Barmouth LL42 1HW

Hangin' Pizzeria | Palm oil free, delicious pizza!
1 Station Rd, Betws-y-Coed LL24 0AE

Olif Restaurant (and B&B) | Spanish tapas with a taste of Wales
Holyhead Rd, Betws-y-Coed LL24 0AY

1085 Bistro | Delicious food **(named after Mt Snowdon's height)**
Padarn Hotel, High Street, Llanberis LL55 4SU

Top Tip: Visit *snowdon.live* to check for weather warnings before heading to Snowdons summit. Conditions can change quickly so keep checking, even into the hours before your hike.

Snowdon

Accommodation

£

Bryn Dinas Camping Pods | 01766 890351
Nant Gwynant, Caernarfon LL55 4NH

Dolafon Guest House | 01286 870993
High St, Llanberis, Caernarfon LL55 4SU

Hendre Mynach Glamping Pods | 01341 280262
Llanaber Rd, Barmouth LL42 1YR

££

Dolffanog Fawr Guest House | 01654 761247
Tal-y-llyn, Tywyn LL36 9AJ

Glyntwrog House | 07920 835346
Dinas Hill, Betws-y-Coed LL24 0SG

Tyn-yr-Onnen Farm Pods & Lodges | 01286 650281
Waunfawr, Caernarfon LL55 4AX

£££

Royal Oak Hotel | 01690 710219
Holyhead Rd, Betws-y-Coed LL24 0AY

Hotel Portmeirion | 01766 770000
Penrhyndeudraeth LL48 6ER

Plas Dinas Country House | 01286 830214
Bontnewydd, Caernarfon LL54 7YF

A Weekend Itinerary...

Day	Morning	Afternoon	Evening
Friday	Arrive in Snowdonia	Visit the National Slate Museum	Dinner at 1085 Bistro
Saturday	Take the Watkin Path to the Waterfalls	Wander around Betws-y-Coed	Enjoy tapas at Olif Restaurant
Sunday	Explore Portmeirion	Discover Harlech Castle	Travel home

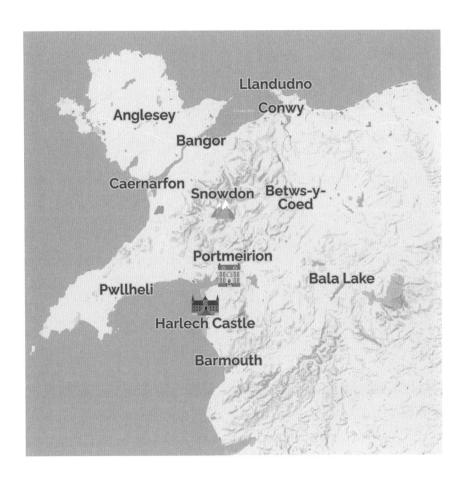

Best way to explore Snowdonia...

You'll need a car to travel from destination to destination across Snowdonia as the park stretches for 823 square miles. Alternatively, you could travel by train and stay in one location *(such as Betws-y-Coed or Barmouth)* for the entirety of your weekend.

 Did you know?

Snowdonia is the third largest National Park in the UK. Cairngorms National Park in Scotland is the largest and the Lake District National Park is the second largest.

Top picks for slowing down...

Betws-y-Coed
LL24 0AH

Fancy a relaxed afternoon pottering around independent stores, art galleries and enjoying locally sourced food in a range of cafés and pubs? Then head to the quaint village of Betws-y-Coed and enjoy its magical setting, which is enhanced by the surrounding Gwydyr Forest.

Snowdon Mountain Railway
Llanberis LL55 4TU

If you don't fancy the hike up Snowdon then take the incredibly scenic journey along the Snowdon Mountain Railway, all the way to the summit. The railway is open from mid-March until the end of October and it's recommended to book online in advance as it's a popular activity!

Barmouth
LL42 1LX

Fancy a day at the seaside? Barmouth is a charming town with a large beach, quaint harbour and delicious fish, chips and ice cream. Take a boat trip from the harbour, head for some fun at the amusement arcades or mooch around the quirky shops, followed with a stop at Knickerbockers Ice Cream Parlour!

Unique things to see & do...

Portmeirion
Penrhyndeudraeth, LL48 6ER

Portmeirion is a unique tourist village with gardens that's built in the style of an Italian village and overlooks the stunning coastal scenery of North Wales. The enchanting village makes for a great morning or afternoon visit, where you can shop, eat, stay or even visit the spa. Entry prices vary depending on the season.

Harlech Castle
Harlech LL46 2YH

A UNESCO World Heritage Site! This epic 13th century fortress overlooks the Irish Sea and sits amongst a backdrop of Snowdonia's rugged peaks. It's open all year-round, tickets can be purchased on arrival, and it provides a mighty place to explore for an hour or two. *(If you loved Harlech, check out the nearby Conwy Castle).*

Barmouth

Portmeirion

Snowdon Mountain Railway

Top picks for adventure seekers...

Zip World
Multiple locations

The ultimate day out for adrenaline junkie couples! From the world's fastest zipline taking you over Penrhyn Quarry at over 100mph, to the UK's only alpine coaster at the Zip World Fforest in Betws-y-Coed. Zip World offer multiple activities to get the heart racing! Booking is essential.

Bala Lake (Llyn Tegid)
LL23 7SW

Lake Bala is Wales' largest natural lake. Experience several outdoor activities on offer including kayaking, climbing and gorge walking, or enjoy a 9-mile return journey on the Bala Lake Railway where you can take in views of Snowdonia and the lake itself. The historic market town of Bala is also worth a visit.

Snowdon Hike (Yr Wyddfa)
LL55 4UL

Standing at a whopping 1,085 metres, Snowdon is one of the UK's most popular mountain climbs. With six main walking paths and absolutely spectacular views (on a clear day), it's a hikers paradise! Always check the weather, wear suitable clothing and take plenty to drink and eat – it's no walk in the park!

Budget-friendly finds...

Watkin Path Waterfalls
Nant Gwynant LL55 4NH

Follow the Watkin Path towards the summit of Snowdon for around 25-30 minutes and you'll reach a set of magnificent waterfalls. Cross over a small bridge to find deep pools of Instagrammable turquoise blue water. Those brave enough to bare the fresh mountain water will be rewarded with an unforgettable experience!

National Slate Museum
Llanberis LL55 4TY

Head to the National Slate Museum for something a little different, the museum is housed in the Industrial Victorian Workshops that once serviced and maintained the enormous Dinorwig slate quarry above. It's free to enter and is open all year-round (apart from being closed on Saturdays from November-March).

Our visit to Snowdonia...

Date visited:

We visited...

☐ Betws-y-Coed

☐ Barmouth

☐ Portmeirion

☐ Harlech Castle

☐ Bala Lake (Llyn Tegid)

☐ ....

☐ ....

☐ Snowdon Mountain Railway

☐ Zip World

☐ Snowdon Hike (Yr Wyddfa)

☐ Watkin Path Waterfalls

☐ National Slate Museum

☐ ....

☐ ....

Notes...

....

....

....

....

....

....

Rating: ♡♡♡♡♡

*Our favourite photo
from the weekend*

Date:

Location:

Caption:

Cardiff

The buzzing capital and largest city in Wales! From castles to culture and water sports to pubs, Cardiff seems to tick all the boxes for a perfect weekend away. Pop-up dining, intimate gigs and global sporting events - it all seems to be going on! If you time your trip right, you'll be able to watch a fierce game of rugby or perhaps even a boxing match at the Principality Stadium *(if that's your thing!?)*.

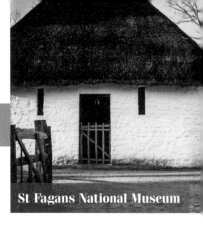

St Fagans National Museum

Romance ♥♥♥♥♡
Food & Drink ♥♥♥♥♡
Things To See ♥♥♥♥♡
Natural Beauty ♥♥♥♡♡

Cardiff Castle

Drive Time to Cardiff
From London | 3 hours
From Manchester | 4 hours
From Newcastle | 6 hours
From Birmingham | 3 hours
From Plymouth | 3 hours

Train Duration to Cardiff
From London | 2 hours
From Manchester | 3.5 hours
From Newcastle | 6 hours
From Birmingham | 2.5 hours
From Plymouth | 4 hours

Best Time to Visit...
Sporting Season - If you're looking for a weekend filled with a buzzing atmosphere then head to Cardiff on a match weekend (if you fancy something a little quieter then avoid those dates!).
Winter - Cardiff at Christmas is magical and romantic, head to Cardiff Castle for ice skating and Christmas markets.

Best Places to Eat & Drink...

The Busy Teapot | Delicious breakfast and lunch
27 Glebe Street, Penarth CF64 1EE

Fresh the Baguette Bar | The best sandwich in Cardiff
32 Royal Arcade, Cardiff CF10 1AE

Vivo Amigo Cardiff | Mexican meets Indian **(lunch & dinner)**
138 Whitchurch Road, Cardiff CF14 3LZ

Purple Poppadom | Award-winning Indian cuisine
185a Cowbridge Road East, Cardiff CF11 9AJ

Heaneys | Independent, fine dining bar & restaurant
6-10 Romilly Crescent, Pontcanna, Cardiff CF11 9NR

Top Tip: Boozy night together? Head to Clwb Ifor Bach for live music! End your night with a visit to the famous 'chippy lane' (Caroline Street) to grab some fast food.

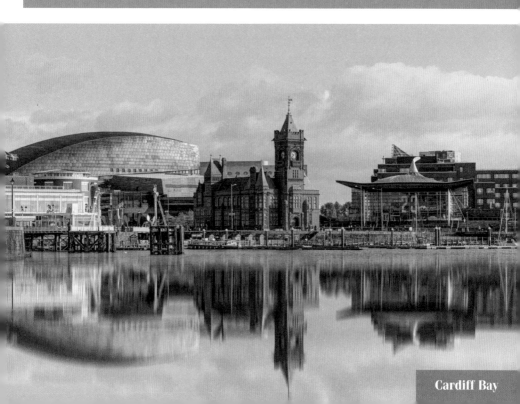

Cardiff Bay

Accommodation

£	**Sleeperz Hotel Cardiff** | 0292 047 8747 Station Approach, Saunders Road, Cardiff CF10 1RH **Premier Inn Cardiff City Centre** | 0333 777 3981 Helmont House, 10 Churchill Way, Cardiff CF10 2HE **Travelodge Cardiff Atlantic Wharf** | 0871 984 6424 Hemingway Road, Cardiff CF10 4JY
££	**The Coal Exchange Hotel** | 0292 199 1904 Mount Stuart Square, Cardiff CF10 5FQ **The Parkgate Hotel** | 0292 274 5595 Westgate Street, Cardiff CF10 1DA **Staybridge Suites Cardiff** | 0800 083 1441 Longueil Close Atlantic Wharf, Cardiff CF10 4EE
£££	**voco St. David's Cardiff** | 0292 045 4045 Havannah Street, Cardiff CF10 5SD **Hilton Cardiff** | 0292 064 6300 Kingsway, Greyfriars Rd Cardiff CF10 3HH **Parador 44** | 0292 002 0039 14-15 Quay St, Cardiff CF10 1DD

A Weekend Itinerary...

Day	Morning	Afternoon	Evening
Friday	Arrive in Cardiff	Explore Cardiff Bay	Enjoy dinner and drinks at Heaneys
Saturday	Visit St Fagans National Museum	See whats on offer at Cardiff Market	Catch a show at the Wales Millennium Centre
Sunday	Explore Cardiff Castle	Wander around Bute Park	Travel home

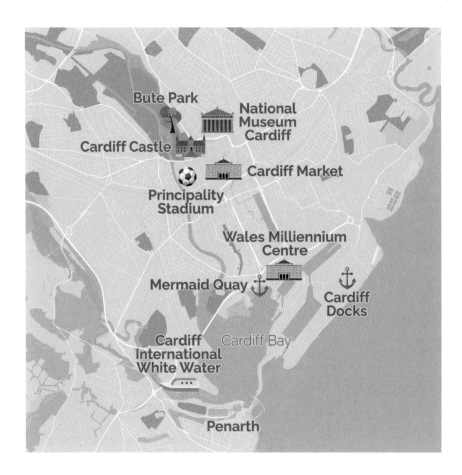

Best way to explore Cardiff...

Cardiff is a fairly compact city; however, if you're walking from Cardiff Castle to Cardiff Bay *(for example)*, you're looking at a 1-hour walk. Purchasing a hop-on hop-off sightseeing bus ticket or hiring e-scooters could be an alternative option for a quicker way to explore the city.

 Did you know?

The famous children's author, Roald Dahl, was born in Cardiff. Known for books such as *'Charlie and the Chocolate Factory', 'James & the Giant Peach'* and *'Matilda'.*

Top picks for slowing down...

Cardiff Bay
Mermaid Quay, CF10 5BZ

A former industrial site that has been re-imagined over the last 30 years to become Europe's largest waterfront development. Mermaid Quay is a must visit spot filled with restaurants & cafés providing exceptional views over the water. Why not jump on one of the many boat rides and view the bay from a different perspective?

Wales Millennium Centre
Bute Place, CF10 5AL

If you fancy an evening of theatre *(whether that be a musical, opera, ballet or stand-up comedy - just to name a few)* head to Wales' national home for the performing arts. Located in Cardiff Bay, this spectacular venue attracts performers from all over the world. Purchase tickets for your preferred show online.

Unique things to see & do...

Cardiff Castle
Castle St, CF10 3RB

History lovers can explore 2,000 years of history at Cardiff Castle, whilst enjoying panoramic views over the city. Guided tours are available for an additional fee. If you don't fancy heading inside you can enjoy the outer green space *(The Public Square)* free of charge, along with gift shop and café.

Cardiff Market
St Mary's Street, CF10 1AU

St Mary's street has a number of Edwardian and Victorian shopping arcades packed with an array of cafés and independent shops. The entrance to Cardiff Market is also on St Mary's street and is home to two floors of stalls from vinyl records to bakeries *(don't forget to grab a Welsh Cake)*.

St Fagans National Museum
St Fagans, CF5 6XB

A unique open-air museum that showcases over 50 buildings from throughout Welsh history that have been taken down from their original sites and re-erected here. Entry is free! The Museum stands in the grounds of St Fagans Castle and gardens, another place you might want to visit.

Cardiff Market

Bute Park

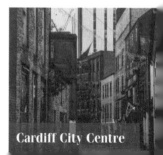
Cardiff City Centre

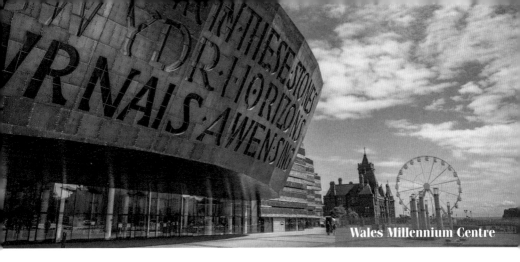
Wales Millennium Centre

Top picks for adventure seekers...

Cardiff International White Water
Cardiff Bay, CF11 0SY

If you're looking for adventure head to the CIWW Hub in Cardiff Bay! There are several experiences on offer including white water rafting, hot dogging, kayaking, paddleboarding and surf & bodyboarding within the indoor wave section. Gorge Walking is also on offer; however, it's located at Neath Valley. Pre-book online.

Budget-friendly finds...

Bute Park
North Road, CF10 3ER

Once the grounds of Cardiff Castle, this 130-acre public park sits in the heart of the city. Take a walk along one of the many trails *(including along the River Taff and the sculpture trail)* and discover the many wildlife species that call the park home, or rent a bike from Pedal Power. There's also cafés and a visitors centre.

National Museum of Wales
Cathays Park, CF10 3NP

Gain a better understanding of the evolution of Wales at this free-to-visit gallery and museum, that showcases a range of art and science displays *(covering all things Welsh, from the Big Bang to the modern-day)*. They often host events, so take a look online before visiting to see what's on.

Penarth
Penarth, CF64 3AU

A short 20-minute*(ish)* drive from Cardiff centre sits this charming seaside town with a Victorian Pier, esplanade and marina. Cosmeston Lakes Country Park and Medieval Village are located in between the coast and the town centre and boast over 100 hectares filled with all kinds of wildlife.

137

Our visit to Cardiff...

We visited...

☐ Cardiff Bay   ☐ Wales Millennium Centre

☐ Cardiff Castle   ☐ St Fagans National Museum

☐ Cardiff Market   ☐ Cardiff International WW

☐ Bute Park   ☐ National Museum of Wales

☐ Penarth   ☐ ....

☐ ....   ☐ ....

☐ ....   ☐ ....

Notes...

....

....

....

....

....

....

Rating: ♡♡♡♡♡

*Our favourite photo
from the weekend*

Date:

Location:

Caption:

Midlands

Peak District

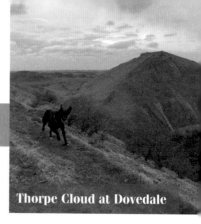

Best For: Walks, nature, outdoor adventure, quaint villages & cosy pubs.

Situated in the heart of England, this 555 square mile national park is a dream for outdoor lovers. Spend the weekend exploring stunning country homes, enjoy a picnic with jaw-dropping views or embark on a leisurely stroll through some of its charming villages. For the adrenaline junkies out there, the Peaks have several extreme climbing, mountain biking and wild outdoor pursuits to tackle. Home to some of England's finest natural beauty, the Peak District offers a perfect escape from the busy hustle and bustle of daily life.

Thorpe Cloud at Dovedale

Romance ♥♥♥♥♡
Food & Drink ♥♥♥♡♡
Things To See ♥♥♥♡♡
Natural Beauty ♥♥♥♥♥

Thor's Cave

Drive Time to Bakewell
From London | 4 hours
From Manchester | 2 hours
From Newcastle | 3.5 hours
From Birmingham | 2 hours
From Cardiff | 4 hours

Train Duration to Bakewell
From London | 3.5 hours
From Manchester | 2 hours
From Newcastle | 3.5 hours
From Birmingham | 3 hours
From Cardiff | 4.5 hours

Best Time to Visit...
Summer - Visit between May and September if you want to spend time outdoors. These months offer the longest daylight and the best chance of dry weather.
Winter - The weather might be grey and wet; however, you can experience the Christmas markets on offer within the quaint towns and villages, and then relax by a roaring fire in a cosy country pub.

Best Places to Eat & Drink...

The Maynard | Sunday Roast in a country house
Main Rd, Grindleford, Hope Valley S32 2HE

1530 The Restaurant | Italian food in an authentic setting
1627 Cross St, Castleton, Hope Valley S33 8WH

Carriages | Experience dinner in a train-turned-restaurant
A515, A5012, Newhaven, Buxton SK17 0DU

Curry Cottage at Lovers Leap | Indian cuisine
The Dl, Stoney Middleton, Hope Valley S32 4TF

Fischer's at Baslow Hall | Michelin Star food in a listed manor house
Calver Rd, Baslow, Bakewell DE45 1RR

Top Tip: If you wish to hike to the highest point in the Peak District then head to Kinder Scout (measuring 2,086ft, that's 636 metres). You'll be treated to unforgettable views, unique moorland and the picturesque Kinder Downfall waterfall.

Chatsworth House

Accommodation

£

The Shoulder of Mutton | 0143 362 0427
Church Street Cottage, Bradwell, Hope Valley S33 9HJ

Blossom House | 0129 887 2985
Queen St, Tideswell, Buxton SK17 8JZ

Farmyard Inn | 0162 963 6221
Youlgreave, Bakewell DE45 1UW

££

Robin Hood Farm | 0124 658 2868
Old Brampton Road, Baslow, Bakewell DE45 1PU

Rutland Arms Hotel | 0162 981 2812
The Square, Bakewell DE45 1BT

The Plough Inn | 0143 365 0319
The Plough Inn, Leadmill Bridge, Hathersage S32 1BA

£££

Losehill House Hotel & Spa | 0143 362 1219
Lose Hill Lane, Edale Rd, Hope Valley S33 6AF

Fischer's Baslow Hall | 0124 658 3259
Calver Rd, Baslow, Bakewell DE45 1RR

The Peacock at Rowsley | 0162 973 3518
Bakewell Rd, Rowsley, Matlock DE4 2EB

A Weekend Itinerary...

Day	Morning	Afternoon	Evening
Friday	Arrive in the Peak District	Explore Dovedale or Thor's Cave	Dinner at Carriages
Saturday	Visit Chatsworth House	Wander around Bakewell	Enjoy Michelin Star food at Fischer's at Baslow Hall
Sunday	Watch the sunrise at Mam Tor	Take a tour of Treak Cliff Cavern	Travel home

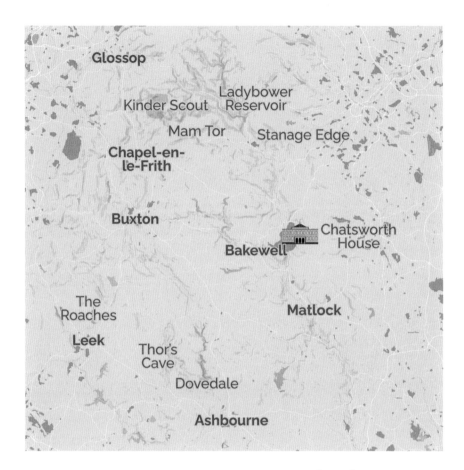

Best way to explore the Peak District...

Undoubtedly, the best way to explore the Peak District is by car. However, whilst it is possible to travel via public train and bus, the timetables are reduced during weekends, making it more challenging. Worth considering, is the open-top hop on hop off bus tour that travels around the Bakewell area.

 Did you know?

There are 26,000 miles of dry stone wall in the Peak District. That's the equivalent to a wall around the Earth. The National Park also reaches into five counties; Derbyshire, Cheshire, Staffordshire, Yorkshire and Greater Manchester.

Top picks for slowing down...

Losehill House Spa
Lose Hill Lane, Edale Road, Hope Valley S33 6AF

Book a half-day spa experience and admire the views across the Hope Valley whilst relaxing in the indoor heated pool, as well as sampling the sauna and outdoor hot tub. You'll be able to choose a 50-minute spa treatment, which is included within your experience, along with a two-course lunch.

Unique things to see & do...

Chatsworth House
Bakewell DE45 1PP

Visit this magnificent stately home and its vast 105-acre gardens, situated on the bank of the river Derwent. They host a wide range of events throughout the year. Buy a ticket to tour the house and gardens (*pre-booking is recommended*) or pull out a blanket and admire the house from across the river.

Thor's Cave
Wetton Car Park, Carr Lane, Wetton, Ashbourne DE6 2AF

Follow the scenic Manifold Way footpath until you reach the impressive natural cavern that's set within a steep limestone crag towering above you! Take care as you climb the steep slope towards the arch-shaped entrance into the cave. Why not reward yourself afterwards with a slice of cake at the Wetton Tea room?

Dovedale & Milldale
Ashbourne DE6 2BD

Soak in the fresh air and the sound of the River Dove, trickling through the scenic valley. Head for the stepping stones or climb to the top of Thorpe Cloud for epic views. If Dovedale happens to be busy, why not park in Ilam and walk across or visit Milldale instead (*also on the River Dove)*, which receives a fraction of the visitors?

Ladybower Reservoir

Mam Tor

The Roaches

Top picks for adventure seekers...

Treak Cliff Cavern
Buxton Road, Castleton,
Hope Valley S33 8WP

A fascinating underground world of stalactites, stalagmites, rocks and minerals – including the unique blue john stone *(one of only two locations in the world where these stones can be found!)*. Pre-book a self-guided tour online. A unique 'blue john stone' craftsman experience is available January – March.

Mam Tor
Hope Valley S33 8WA

Hike the stone surfaced footpath and be rewarded with some staggering views over Edale Valley and beyond! It's a popular spot to climb and watch the sunrise *(romantic eh!)*. It's no wonder Mam Tor was ranked 10th in the National Trust/ITVs 'Britain's 100 favourite walks' in 2018.

The Roaches
Leek ST13 8UQ

Situated in the Staffordshire part of the Peak District, the Roaches is loved by walkers and climbers alike for its craggy rocks and gritstone edges. Take a scenic walk amongst the impressive landscape - if you're feeling daring, why not have a go at climbing? Climbing courses are available with local companies.

Budget-friendly finds...

Bakewell
DE45 1DS

This charming market town *(home to the famous Bakewell tart)* is surrounded by epic countryside and situated on the River Wye - think cosy tea rooms, striking stone buildings, a charming arched bridge, historic almshouses, markets and more. Make sure to visit the Love Locks Bridge and add your own padlock!

Ladybower Reservoir
S33 0AQ

Located within the Upper Derwent Valley, this large reservoir is surrounded by countryside and woodland and offers the true meaning of escapism. You could take one of the many scenic walks *(head to Bamford Edge for an epic viewpoint!)* or relax with a picnic and soak in your surroundings.

147

Our visit to the Peak District...

We visited...

☐ Losehill House Spa   ☐ Chatsworth House

☐ Thor's Cave   ☐ Dovedale & Milldale

☐ Treak Cliff Cavern   ☐ Mam Tor

☐ The Roaches   ☐ Bakewell

☐ Ladybower Reservoir   ☐ ....

☐ ....   ☐ ....

☐ ....

Notes...

....

....

....

....

....

....

Rating: ♡♡♡♡♡

*Our favourite photo
from the weekend*

Date:

Location:

Caption:

Lincoln

Minster Yard

A beautiful city home to some of England's oldest historic landmarks, step back in time with a charming visit to Lincoln. Escape into its cobbled streets, quaint shops and homey cafés during a cosy, romantic weekend away. From its iconic cathedral to its many delicious eateries to the scenic surrounding landscapes, all within a few miles, Lincoln combines history with convenience for a truly wholesome couples' getaway.

Romance ♥♥♥♥♡
Food & Drink ♥♥♥♥♡
Things To See ♥♥♥♡♡
Natural Beauty ♥♥♥♡♡

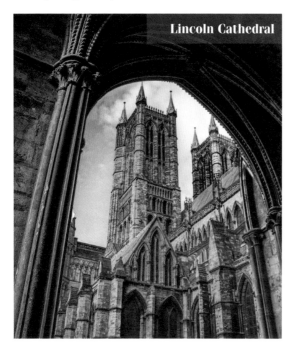
Lincoln Cathedral

Drive Time to Lincoln
From London | 3 hours
From Manchester | 2.5 hours
From Newcastle | 3 hours
From Birmingham | 2 hours
From Cardiff | 4 hours

Train Duration to Lincoln
From London | 2 hours
From Manchester | 3 hours
From Newcastle | 3.5 hours
From Birmingham | 2.5 hours
From Cardiff | 5 hours

Best Time to Visit...
Spring - Visit from March to May for a chance to see Lincoln in bloom and before the summer holiday crowds arrive.
Autumn - With its cobbled streets and quaint shops, Lincoln transforms into a cosy retreat from late September to early November.

Best Places to Eat & Drink...

Rising Café Lincoln | Charity-focused cosy café
Alive Lincoln Central, Lincoln LN1 1XD

Bunty's Tearoom | Homemade cakes and tea
18 Steep Hill, Lincoln LN2 1LT

Slow Rise | Vegetarian Neapolitan pizza
8-12 St. Martins Lane, Lincoln LN2 1HY

Lawson's Bar & Bistro | Modern fine dining
8-9 The Strait, Lincoln LN2 1JD

The Electric | Swanky sky bar overlooking the waterfront
Brayford Wharf North DoubleTree by Hilton, Lincoln LN1 1YW

Top Tip: Lincoln is a great spot for real ale lovers, take the 'Lincoln Ale Trail'. There are 24 venues to visit, from the historic pubs in the Bailgate area to the vibrant bars on the Brayford Waterfront.

Lincoln City

Accommodation

£

The Lincoln Hotel | 0152 252 0348
Eastgate, Lincoln LN2 1PN

Travelodge Lincoln City Centre | 0871 984 6543
16 Tentercroft Street, Lincoln LN5 7DB

Brayford Guest House | 0152 288 5007
79 Carholme Road, Lincoln LN1 1RT

££

The Tower Hotel | 0152 252 9999
38 Westgate, Lincoln LN1 3BD

Cathedral View Guest House | 0152 2537 469
6 Eastgate, Lincoln LN2 1QA

The Rest Hotel | 0152 224 7888
55a Steep Hill, Lincoln LN2 1LR

£££

The Poplars | 0152 251 0170
The Poplars Beaumont Fee, Lincoln LN1 1EZ

The White Hart | 0152 252 6222
Bailgate, Lincoln LN1 3AR

The Old Palace Lodge | 0152 258 1447
Christ's Hospital Terrace, Lincoln LN2 1LY

A Weekend Itinerary...

Day	Morning	Afternoon	Evening
Friday	Arrive in Lincoln	Explore Lincoln Castle	Dinner and drinks at Lawson's Bar & Bistro
Saturday	Lincoln Cathedral	Steep Hill & Bunty's Tearoom	Drinks at The Electric & a show at the New Theatre Royal
Sunday	Museum of Lincoln-shire Life	Brayford Waterfront	Travel home

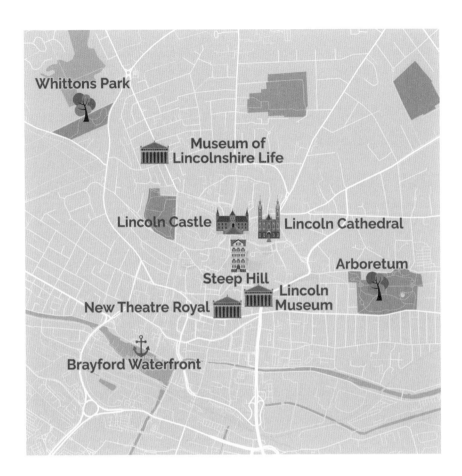

Best way to explore Lincoln...

Due to its small size and most attractions being located centrally, Lincoln is the perfect city to explore on foot. There are open tour buses available and a park & ride service into the city centre too.

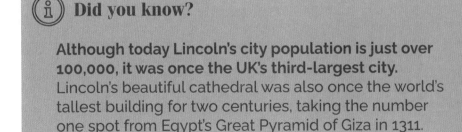

(i) **Did you know?**

Although today Lincoln's city population is just over 100,000, it was once the UK's third-largest city. Lincoln's beautiful cathedral was also once the world's tallest building for two centuries, taking the number one spot from Egypt's Great Pyramid of Giza in 1311.

Top picks for slowing down...

New Theatre Royal
Clasketgate, LN2 1JJ

Entertaining the people of Lincoln since 1893, the New Theatre Royal is the perfect sanctuary on a rainy day. From live music, plays, comedy shows and opera, there are tonnes of choices at this theatre. For true thespians, you can even sign up to a backstage tour where you'll uncover all the behind-the-scenes secrets!

Unique things to see & do...

Lincoln Cathedral
Minster Yard, LN2 1PX

One of Europe's most iconic churches and a must-visit attraction. Its striking gothic style architecture has been the backdrop within Hollywood blockbusters *(including The Da Vinci Code and Napoleon)*. Make sure to join the 'floor tour' *(free with admission)* and sign up for one of the other tours to learn more about this historic landmark.

Brayford Waterfront
Brayford Wharf North, LN1 1YZ

England's oldest inland harbour, Brayford Waterfront offers a great choice of eateries, bars and entertainment venues. If you're visiting in the summer, dining outside overlooking the water is a must. For a romantic afternoon on the water, hop aboard the Brayford Belley to see Lincoln from a whole new perspective.

Lincoln Castle
Castle Square, LN1 3AA

Home to one of the four original copies of Magna Carta *(a legal document dating back to 1215)* and almost 1000 years of tales, Lincoln Castle is an amazing day out for history buffs. Not for the faint-hearted, parts of the castle have a gruesome past and guided tours are the best way to hear all the details!

Steep Hill

Lincoln Castle

Lincoln Cathedral

Top picks for adventure seekers...

Jump Inc Lincoln
Sunningdale Trading Estate,
Unit 1, Dixon Cl, LN6 7UB

In the wise words of The Pointer Sisters, 'Jump, jump for my love' at Lincoln's Jump Inc., an indoor trampoline, ninja course and inflatable park extravaganza. Open 9am - 6:30pm over the weekends, this is an adrenaline-fuelled date spot you both won't be forgetting anytime soon! Pre-book online.

Gridline Racing
Dunford Road, LN5 8HF

Decide once and for all who's the better driver at Gridline Racing, Lincoln's indoor go-karting centre. The multi-storey circuit will have you both drifting, speeding and hopefully not crashing around each twist and turn. Make sure to pre-book for this one and you must arrive 40 minutes before your slot.

Budget-friendly finds...

Steep Hill
Steep Hill, LN2 1LU

If you're both into your photography or enjoy a good Insta selfie/photoshoot *(no judgement here)*, Steep Hill is an area you'll want to explore. Dotted with picturesque shops, tea rooms and pubs, it feels a little like stepping onto the set of Harry Potter's Diagon Alley when wandering Steep Hill!

Museum of Lincolnshire Life
Burton Road, LN1 3LY

Free to enter, the museum celebrates the rich and diverse history of Lincolnshire. With exhibitions covering from 1750 to the present day, it's home to an authentic WW1 tank, known as 'Daphne' and a Victorian printing press. After an hour or so of learning about Lincolnshire life, grab a coffee from the café and peruse the giftshop.

Hartsholme County Park
377 Skellingthorpe Road, LN6 0EY

Head just two miles outside of Lincoln and you'll find over 200 acres of pristine open space at Hartsholme County Park. With Victorian landscaped gardens, a large reservoir, woodlands and grasslands to explore, it's a picture-perfect spot for an afternoon wander and picnic together.

Our visit to Lincoln...

We visited...

☐ New Theatre Royal

☐ Brayford Waterfront

☐ Jump Inc Lincoln

☐ Gridline Racing

☐ Hartsholme County Park

☐ ....

☐ ....

☐ Lincoln Cathedral

☐ Lincoln Castle

☐ Museum of Lincolnshire Life

☐ Steep Hill

☐ ....

☐ ....

☐ ....

Notes...

....

....

....

....

....

....

Rating: ♡♡♡♡♡

156

*Our favourite photo
from the weekend*

Date:

Location:

Caption:

East of England

Norfolk

Cromer Pier

Norfolk is a diverse county blessed with beautiful countryside, epic coastline and rich culture. Often overlooked, this part of East England is known for endless skies, sandy beaches and a web of waterways. We've grouped together some of its 'top' destinations including Norwich city and the Broads National Park which make for one mighty couples weekend away! Adventurers, wildlife lovers and culture vultures will especially love Norfolk!

Romance ♥♥♥♡♡
Food & Drink ♥♥♥♡♡
Things To See ♥♥♥♥♡
Natural Beauty ♥♥♥♥♥

Wells-next-the-Sea

Drive Time to Norwich
From London | 3 hours
From Manchester | 4.5 hours
From Newcastle | 5 hours
From Birmingham | 3 hours
From Cardiff | 4.5 hours

Train Duration to Norwich
From London | 2 hours
From Manchester | 4.5 hours
From Newcastle | 4.5 hours
From Birmingham | 4 hours
From Cardiff | 4.5 hours

Best Time to Visit...
As with all coastal and countryside locations Norfolk is best when the sun is shining, however, it can be enjoyed at any time of year. Norwich specifically is host to many festivals throughout the year – such as the Sundown Festival in August, the Science Festival during February half term and The City of Ale Festival from May to June - so check out what's on before you visit *(you might want to join in or avoid the crowds!)*.

Best Places to Eat & Drink...

Ground | Good coffee, sweet bakes & delicious sausage rolls
42 Staithe Street, Wells-next-the-Sea NR23 1AG

Wells Crab House | Highly rated seafood restaurant
38-40 Freeman St, Wells-next-the-Sea NR23 1BA

Slice + Dice | Board game café and bar **(over 300 games!)**
10-12 St Benedicts St, Norwich NR2 4AG

Figbar | Indulgent dessert & wine bar
23 St John Maddermarket, Norwich NR2 1DN

The Blue Oyster | Small plates, stonebakes pizza & more
42A King St, Great Yarmouth NR30 2PN

Top Tip: Be sure to pack some binoculars, Norfolk is known to be an incredible location for bird spotting. The nature reserves at Titchwell, Cley and Holkham are particularly popular with bird watchers.

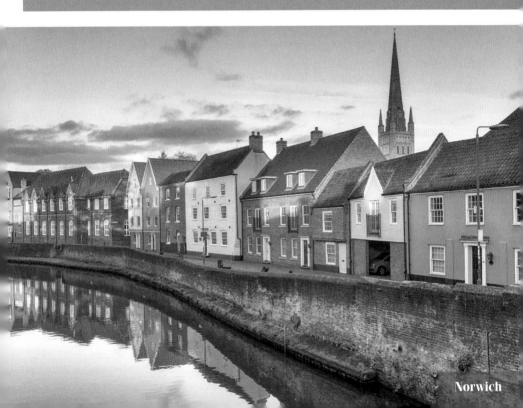

Norwich

Accommodation

North Norfolk Glamping (My Mini Break) | 0789 799 6507
Holt Hollow, Edgefield Hill Road, Holt, Norfolk NR25 6SP

Sandcliff Guest House | 0126 351 2888
37 Runton Road, Cromer NR27 9AS

Andover House Hotel | 0149 384 3490
27-30 Camperdown, Great Yarmouth NR30 3JB

The Globe Inn Hotel | 0132 871 0206
The Buttlands, Wells-Next-The-Sea, Norfolk NR23 1EU

The George Hotel | 0160 3617 841
Arlington Lane, Newmarket Road, Norwich NR2 2DA

Imperial Hotel | 0149 384 2000
13-15 North Drive, Great Yarmouth NR30 1EQ

The Manor Coastal Hotel & Inn | 0126 367 9011
The Quay, Blakeney NR25 7ND

Park Farm Hotel | 0160 3810 264
Norwich Road, Hethersett, Norwich NR9 3DL

The Clubhouse at Fritton Lake | 0149 348 4008
Beccles Road, Fritton, Great Yarmouth, Norfolk NR31 9HA

A Weekend Itinerary...

Day	Morning	Afternoon	Evening
Friday	Arrive in Norfolk	Take a ride on the North Norfolk Railway	Enjoy some delicious seafood at Wells Crab House
Saturday	Find your way around Priory Maze & Gardens	Go crabbing in Wells-next-the-Sea	Dinner and game night at Slice + Dice
Sunday	Explore Norwich City *(preferably a full day)*	Or explore the Broads National Park *(preferably a full day)*	Travel home

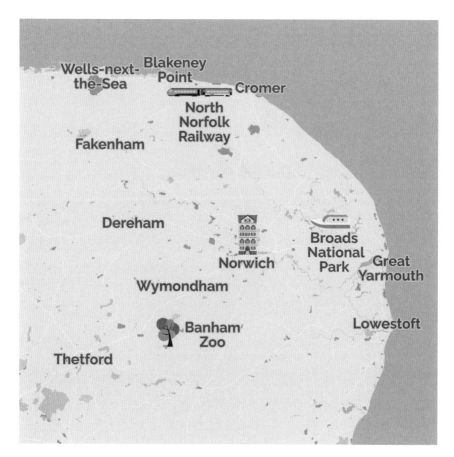

Best way to explore Norfolk...

You'll need a car to travel from destination to destination across Norfolk as the county stretches for over 2,000 square miles. Alternatively, you could travel by train and stay in one location *(such as Cromer, Great Yarmouth or Norwich)* for the entirety of your weekend. Norwich has a hop-on hop-off bus you could use to get around.

 Did you know?

The Norfolk Broads were a man-made accident. They were formed by the flooding of medieval peat excavations which provided fuel to Norwich and Great Yarmouth. As the sea levels began to rise, the pits began to flood. By the end of the 14th century, the pits were abandoned and the Broads were formed.

Top picks for slowing down...

North Norfolk Railway

Sheringham Station, Station Approach, Sheringham NR26 8RA

Sit back and relax as you steam through the scenic countryside onboard a vintage train. The eight-mile journey will take you from the seaside resort of Sheringham to the Georgian town of Holt. You could even book a special experience to enjoy together whilst onboard, from fine dining to a murder mystery!

Unique things to see & do...

Broads National Park

Wroxham, NR12 8SX

We could fill an entire section with things to do across this 117 square mile park – woodlands, waterways, wildlife and so much more! Hire a boat, kayak or canoe or take a trip on a river cruiser. Prefer staying on dry land? Walk or cycle the many riverside pathways or explore Wroxham village, known as the 'capital' of the Broads.

Cromer

Cromer Pier, NR27 9HE

Situated on the north Norfolk coast, Cromer is a traditional seaside destination most recognised for its Grade II listed pier, which homes a lifeboat station and the Pavilion Theatre. Why not see if you can catch one of the theatre's variety shows or head to one of Cromer's museums?

Banham Zoo

Kenninghall Road, Banham, Norwich NR16 2HE

Animal lovers? Spend the day at Banham Zoo, set within 50 acres of Norfolk parkland. Highlights include the Giraffe House, Penguin Cove and Sea Lion Bay. Is it a special occasion? You could book an animal experience for an up-close interaction. Make sure to pre-book your tickets online.

Priory Maze & Gardens

Cromer Road, Beeston Regis, Sheringham NR26 8SF

Looking for something fun and a little different? Work together to find your way through the 7-foot-tall maze, set within the tranquil 10 acre of gardens. There's also several walking trails and a café to enjoy, or why not take a picnic if the weather's playing ball? There's no need to pre-book you can just turn up.

Broads National Park (Norfolk Broads)

Wells-next-the-Sea

Blakeney Point

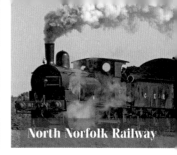
North Norfolk Railway

Top picks for adventure seekers...

Blakeney Point Boat Trips
Multiple locations

Discover Blakeney Point *(home to England's largest grey seal colony!)* from the water, a truly special experience to enjoy together. There are several companies offering boat trips to visit the seals and birds in their natural environment, check out Beans Boats, Bishops Boats or Temple Seal Trips online.

Hunstanton Water Sports & Sea Tours
Hunstanton PE36 5BQ

Feeling adventurous? Take a lesson in paddleboarding or kitesurfing with Hunstanton Watersports *(on the North Norfolk coast)*. Please note, they are closed during the winter period. If you'd rather stay dry you could instead head on a seal safari tour with Searles Sea Tours, also based in Hunstanton.

Budget-friendly finds...

Norwich City
Norwich Castle, Castle Street, NR1 3JU

There's lots to see and do within this walled city; Norwich Castle, Norwich Cathedral, several theatres and the Norwich market *(to name a few)*. Escape the busy centre by visiting the Plantation Gardens *(behind the Cathedral)* or head to Mousehole Heath for skyline views of the city – also a romantic spot to watch the sunset!

Wells-next-the-Sea
Wells-next-the-Sea Beach, NR23 1DR

A picturesque harbour town on the north Norfolk coast. Relax together on the sandy beach, go crabbing on the quay, go bird spotting over on the North Point Pools or head for a walk around the nearby Holkham Hall & Estate *(they even have a tree-top ropes course)*.

Great Yarmouth
S Beach Parade, Great Yarmouth NR30 3EH

The ultimate seaside destination - sandy beaches, piers, fairground rides and arcades are plentiful in Great Yarmouth. Explore one of the many museums, such as the Tollhouse Gaol or the Time & Tide Museum. Why not spend an evening watching a show at the Hippodrome Circus Museum?

Our visit to Norfolk...

We visited...

- ☐ North Norfolk Railway
- ☐ Cromer
- ☐ Priory Maze & Gardens
- ☐ Norwich City
- ☐ Wells-next-the-Sea
- ☐ ....
- ☐ ....

- ☐ Broads National Park
- ☐ Banham Zoo
- ☐ Blakeney Point Boat Trips
- ☐ Great Yarmouth
- ☐ Hunstanton Water Sports & Sea Tours
- ☐ ....
- ☐ ....

Notes...

....

....

....

....

....

....

Rating: ♡♡♡♡♡

*Our favourite photo
from the weekend*

Date:

Location:

Caption:

Cambridge

Best For: Sight-seeing, history, shopping & culture.

A thriving, historic university city, Cambridge is the ideal location for a romantic getaway. It's jam-packed with landmarks and attractions to fill your weekend, as well as restaurants and bars to enjoy a special night out together. If you're looking for a slower pace, the city is perfect for a more relaxed break, thanks to its intimate size you can wander the winding cobbled streets from place to place.

Cambridge City

Romance ♥♥♥♥♥
Food & Drink ♥♥♥♥♡
Things To See ♥♥♥♥♡
Natural Beauty ♥♥♥♡♡

Punting on the River Cam

Drive Time to Cambridge
From London | 1.5 hours
From Manchester | 3.5 hours
From Newcastle | 4 hours
From Birmingham | 2 hours
From Cardiff | 3.5 hours

Train Duration to Cambridge
From London | 1 hours
From Manchester | 3.5 hours
From Newcastle | 3.5 hours
From Birmingham | 3 hours
From Cardiff | 3 hours

Best Time to Visit...
Summer - The ideal time to take a trip down the River Cam in one of Cambridge's famous punting boats and view the city's famous University Colleges from a unique perspective.
Autumn - Experience the many walks in and around the city centre in a more comfortable temperature. Why not retreat to one of the city's cosy pubs afterwards?

Best Places to Eat & Drink...

Limoncello Delicatessen & Bistro | Italian restaurant **(lunch & dinner)**
212 Mill Road, Cambridge CB1 3NF

Taj Tandoori | Indian food with top reviews
64 Cherry Hinton Road, Cambridge CB1 7AA

SIX Cambridge | Bar and restaurant serving city centre views
24 Thompsons Lane 6th Flr, The Varsity Hotel, Cambridge CB5 8AQ

The Corner House | Gastropub just outside of the city centre
231 Newmarket Road, Cambridge CB5 8JE

Restaurant 22 | Michelin star restaurant near to the River Cam
22 Chesterton Road, Cambridge CB4 3AX

Top Tip: Visit between spring and autumn and you might spot cattle roaming parks and green spaces *(part of a centuries-old tradition allowing farmers to graze livestock on common spaces).*

Cambridge City

Accommodation

£

Holiday Inn Cambridge | 0371 942 9015
Lakeview Bridge Road, Impington, Cambridge CB24 9PH

Ibis Cambridge Central Station | 0122 332 0960
2 Station Square, Cambridge CB1 2GA

Turing Locke Aparthotel | 0330 174 4221
47 Eddington Avenue, Cambridge CB3 1SE

££

Centennial Hotel | 0122 331 465
63/71 Hills Road, Cambridge CB2 1PG

Hotel du Vin Cambridge | 0122 392 8991
15-19 Trumpington St, Cambridge CB2 1QA

The Fellows House Cambridge | 0122 394 9499
33A Milton Road, Cambridge CB4 1UZ

£££

Gonville Hotel | 0122 336 6611
Gonville Place, Cambridge CB1 1LY

Graduate Cambridge | 0122 3259 988
Granta Place, Mill Ln, Cambridge CB2 1RT

The Varsity Hotel & Spa | 01223 320562
Thompson's Lane, Cambridge CB5 8AQ

A Weekend Itinerary...

Day	Morning	Afternoon	Evening
Friday	Arrive in Cambridge	City centre walking tour	Watch a film at the Arts Picturehouse
Saturday	Visit the All Saints Garden, Art & Craft Market	Punting on the River Cam	Sunset walk up Castle Mound
Sunday	Explore the Kings College Chapel	Visit the Fitzwilliam Museum	Travel home

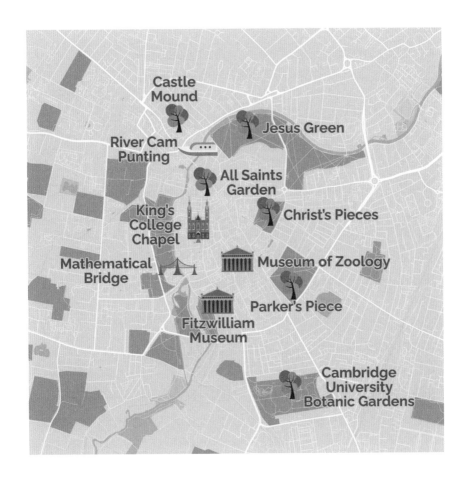

Best way to explore Cambridge...

All of the attractions in Cambridge city centre can be reached on foot so make sure to bring some comfy shoes. If the weather is nice, we'd also recommend hiring a bike and venturing out to some of the pretty surrounding villages.

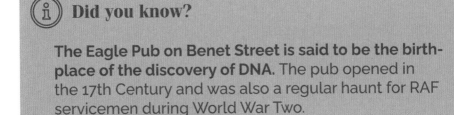

(i) **Did you know?**

The Eagle Pub on Benet Street is said to be the birthplace of the discovery of DNA. The pub opened in the 17th Century and was also a regular haunt for RAF servicemen during World War Two.

Top picks for slowing down...

Punting Tour on the River Cam
Boat station, Jesus Green, CB5 8AG

Explore the city by boat and pass by landmarks such as Trinity College and the Bridge of Sighs along the way. There are several companies running tours, be sure to buy from licenced operators *(such as the Cambridge Punt Company)* online or at the Quayside the Mill Pond and the Jesus Green stations. Look out for the floating bar!

Arts Picturehouse Cinema
38-39 St Andrew's St, CB2 3AR

Visit the Arts Picturehouse for a chilled night in front of the big screen. This traditional cinema shows the latest movies, as well as special showings of musicals and independent films. Arts Picturehouse also plays host to the Cambridge Film Festival which normally takes place each October.

Unique things to see & do...

All Saints Garden, Art & Craft Market
All Saints Garden, Trinity St, CB2 1TQ

If you're looking for a unique souvenir from your trip to Cambridge, this art and craft market may be worth a visit. It's held every Saturday opposite Trinity College and everything on sale is handmade by those who sell it. If you miss this one, there's also a general market open seven days a week at Cambridge Market Square.

Cambridge University Botanic Gardens
1 Brookside, CB2 1JE

Explore the 40-acre Cambridge University Botanic Gardens and its collection of over 8,000 plant species from around the world. There are two entrance gates. Why not stop for a coffee and cake at the Garden Café at the end of your visit *(which is located at Brookside gate)*.

The Cambridge Gin Laboratory
10 Green Street, CB2 3JU

One for the gin lovers! The 'laboratory' offers a variety of 'classes', where you'll learn how to blend and taste gin like a professional. Experiences last one-two hours depending on which you choose. If you don't have time for a class then pop into the shop and grab a bottle to take home. Pre-booking is essential.

Cambridge Botanic Gardens

River Cam

Kings College Chapel

Top picks for culture seekers...

Kings College Chapel
King's Parade, CB2 1ST

Kings College is one of the oldest University of Cambridge buildings and is also considered to be one of the most iconic. Students study here; however, its chapel and gardens are open to the public on a daily basis. Admire the architecture or plan your visit to coincide with one of the daily choral services.

The Fitzwilliam Museum
Trumpington Street, CB2 1RB

A culture lover's dream, the Fitzwilliam houses a world-renowned collection of over half a million pieces of art, paintings and historical artefacts. It's the perfect place to while away an hour or two, particularly as entry is free and you do not need to book tickets in advance.

Budget-friendly finds...

Castle Mound
Castle Street, CB3 0RG

Cambridge is not known to be the most hilly of cities; however, a gentle stroll up Castle Mound will afford you pleasant views over the centre. The site was once home to its own castle but is now a great spot for time spent in nature and a picnic on a warm day. Why not head to the nearby Castle Inn for a pint afterwards?

Footprints Free Walking Tour
11 King's Parade (Fudge Kitchen), CB2 1SJ

There are many different tours you can pay for in Cambridge. However, there are some companies that offer a great experience in exchange for a small voluntary contribution at the end of the tour. Footprints offer a two-hour tour meeting at King's Parade at 11am and 2pm each day. Make sure to book online first though!

Our visit to Cambridge...

We visited...

☐ Arts Picturehouse

☐ Cambridge University
Botantic Gardens

☐ Kings College Chapel

☐ Castle Mound

☐ Footprints Walking Tour

☐ ....

☐ ....

☐ Punting on the River Cam

☐ All Saints Garden, Art
& Craft Market

☐ Cambridge Gin Laboratory

☐ The Fitzwilliam Museum

☐ ....

☐ ....

☐ ....

Notes...

....

....

....

....

....

....

Rating: ♡♡♡♡♡

*Our favourite photo
from the weekend*

Date:

Location:

Caption:

175

Greater London

London

Best For: Attractions, markets, museums, shopping & nightlife.

There's a reason that London is the world's third most visited city. It boasts some of the most magnificent culture, world-renowned attractions and perhaps some of the best food and drink anywhere in Europe *(probably the world)*. In terms of a couples weekends away, London has it all! Whether you want to go sightseeing, clubbing until the early hours, shopping or perhaps watch a West End musical, the possibilities are endless.

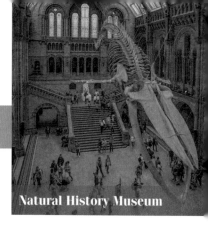

Natural History Museum

Romance ♥♥♥♥♡
Food & Drink ♥♥♥♥♥
Things To See ♥♥♥♥♥
Natural Beauty ♥♥♡♡♡

The London Eye

Drive Time to London
From Manchester | 4 hours
From Newcastle | 5 hours
From Birmingham | 1.5 hours
From Cardiff | 3 hours
From Plymouth | 5 hours

Train Duration to London
From Manchester | 2 hours
From Newcastle | 3 hours
From Birmingham | 2.5 hours
From Cardiff | 2 hours
From Plymouth | 3.5 hours

Best Time to Visit...
London is quite spectacular all year round. There's amazing events, shows and markets on all the time. The quieter time to visit is Spring or Autumn. Winter is especially busy, but you do get the benefit of Christmas markets, incredible lights and Winter Wonderland.

Best Places to Eat & Drink...

Dishoom | Amazing authentic Indian from breakfast to dinner
12 Upper St Martin's Ln, London WC2H 9FB *(6 locations across London)*

Draughts | Boardgame café offering food, craft beers & cocktails
Waterloo (Arch 16 Leake St, SE1 7NN) & Hackney (14 Kingsland High St, E8 2JS)

Crust Bros Waterloo | Award winning pizza restaurant
113 Waterloo Rd, London SE1 8UL

Ikoyi | Michelin star restaurant with a twist on West African food
180 Strand, Temple, London WC2R 1EA

Gaucho | Upmarket steak restaurant with views over Tower Bridge
2 More London Pl, London SE1 2AP *(12 locations across London)*

Top Tip: Avoid upsetting locals and commuters by always standing on the right of escalators and walkways when travelling on the underground.

River Thames

Accommodation

£

The Z Hotel Holborn | 0203 841 0870
75 Kingsway, Camden, London WC2B 6SR

Travelodge London City | 0871 984 6534
20 Middlesex Street, London E1 7EX

Ibis London Blackfriars | 0207 633 2720
49 Blackfriars Road, London SE1 8NZ

££

The Montague on The Gardens | 0207 637 1001
15 Montague St, London WC1B 5BJ

Blakemore Hyde Park | 0207 262 4591
30 Leinster Gardens, London W2 3AN

Park Plaza London Waterloo | 0333 400 6128
6 Hercules Rd, London SE1 7DP

£££

Rubens At The Palace | 0207 834 6600
39 Buckingham Palace Rd, London SW1W 0PS

Pan Pacific | 0207 118 6888
80 Houndsditch, London EC3A 7AB

The Bloomsbury | 0207 347 1000
16-22 Great Russell St, London WC1B 3NN

A Weekend Itinerary...

Day	Morning	Afternoon	Evening
Friday	Arrive in London	Wander around Covent Garden	Catch a show at Theatre Royal Drury Lane
Saturday	Enjoy epic views on the London Eye	Have a scare at London Dungeons	Get competitive at Fairgame Canary Wharf
Sunday	Explore the Natural History Museum	Enjoy afternoon tea at Fortnum & Mason's	Travel home

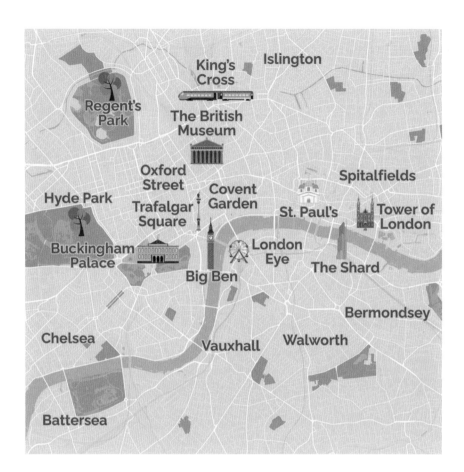

Best way to explore London...

London is a huge city and by far the best way to get around is by using the tube and bus network. Using contactless debit or credit cards is the easiest way to pay. Boris Bikes and E-Scooters are also a fun but slightly hectic way of traversing the capital.

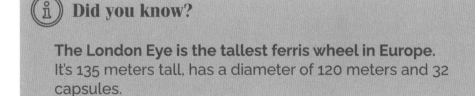

(i) **Did you know?**

The London Eye is the tallest ferris wheel in Europe. It's 135 meters tall, has a diameter of 120 meters and 32 capsules.

Top picks for slowing down...

Theatre Royal Drury Lane
Catherine St, WC2B 5JF

London's West End is packed with amazing theatres home to magical musicals, shows and plays. The 350 year old Theatre Royal, in Covent Garden, is one of the most famous and can be explored through a guided tour offering couples a unique behind the scenes experience.

Afternoon Tea at Fortnum & Mason
Fourth Floor, 181 Piccadilly, St James's, W1A 1ER

Experience a quintessentially British afternoon tea at Fortnum and Masons Diamon Jubilee Tea Salon. Named after Her late Majesty Queen Elizabeth's visit in 2012, when the Tea Room opened. Look forward to freshly baked cakes, precisely cut sandwiches and pots of tea. Definitely pre-book, it's very popular.

Unique things to see & do...

The London Eye
Riverside Building, County Hall, SE1 7PB

Also known as the *'Millennium Wheel'* - It wouldn't be a visit to London without a ride on the iconic London Eye. It's Europe's tallest *'observation wheel'* and offers standard rides, VIP experiences with champagne and private pods. It's worth pre-booking a time slot to avoid queuing at busy times.

London's Markets
Multiple locations

London has so many amazing markets to explore. Some of our favourites are Leadenhall Market *(inspiration for Diagon Alley in Harry Potter)*; Borough Market, London's most famous food market and Camden Market, for a quirky selection of crafts, fashion and all sorts of weird and wonderful things.

Fairgame Canary Wharf
25 Fishermans Walk, E14 4DH

A modern twist on classic fairground games! Have some flirty competition and feel nostalgic at Fairgame. Featuring original fairground games with a 'techy' twist such as 'whac-a-mole' and Skeeball. You can book games and packages in advance. It also has amazing street food and cocktails – ideal for an evening of fun.

Buckingham Palace

Covent Garden

Borough Market

Climb the O2

Top picks for adventure seekers...

The London Dungeon

Riverside Building, County Hall, Westminster Bridge Rd, SE1 7PB

Discover London's gruesome history through an amazing cast of theatrical actors, special effects, stages, scenes and rides. Try not to scream as you re-live the legends of Sweeney Todd, Jack The Ripper, The Plague Doctor and more. Pre-booking tickets will allow you to avoid queues and get the best price.

Climb the O2

Peninsula Square, SE10 0DX

If you're looking for a bit of adrenaline in London then you can strap on a harness and climb the incredible O2 arena, also known as the Millennium dome, for amazing 360 degree views over the City. The whole thing takes around 1.5 hours and it's recommended to do it at sunset.

Budget-friendly finds...

London's Museums

Multiple locations

Incredibly, London has over 40 free museums. Here's a selection of our favourites. The National Gallery *(impressive art collections)*. Imperial War Museum *(from letters of war to machinery)*. National History Museum *(skeletons, fossils and learn about life on earth)*. The Science Museum *(packed with interactive exhibits)*.

Changing of the Guard at Buckingham Palace

Buckingham Palace, SW1A 1AA

Buckingham Palace is a magnificent place to see at any time of day; however, the Changing the Guard is such an experience! This is a formal procedure where the old guard hands over responsibility to the new. This takes place every Monday, Wednesday, Friday and Saturday from 10.45am.

Covent Garden

Covent Garden Piazza, WC2E 7BB

Famous for its street performers, at all times of day, you can wander around the Piazza and find crowds of people stood around a magician, comedian or singer. You never know what performers you might see at Covent Garden, but you can guarantee they'll be putting on one hell of a show. A fabulous way to pass an hour or two.

Our visit to London...

We visited...

☐ The London Eye

☐ London's Markets

☐ Fairgame Canary Wharf

☐ The London Dungeon

☐ Climb the O2

☐ ....

☐ ....

☐ Theatre Royal Drury Lane

☐ Afternoon Tea at Fortnum's

☐ London's Museums

☐ Buckingham Palace

☐ ....

☐ ....

☐ ....

Notes...

....

....

....

....

....

....

Rating: ♡♡♡♡♡

*Our favourite photo
from the weekend*

Date:

Location:

Caption:

South East

Oxford

If you're looking for a romantic weekend get-away full of culture, cosy cafés and cobbled streets, Oxford is the place for you and your partner. Thanks to its intimate size, many of the city's historic attractions can be enjoyed during a weekend away. Try your hand at punting on the River Cherwell, or if you're visiting in the winter, explore the city's many quaint shops before cosying up in front of a local pub's crackling fire.

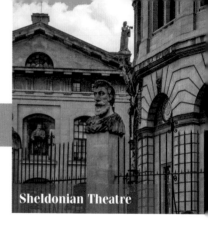

Sheldonian Theatre

Romance ♥♥♥♥♥
Food & Drink ♥♥♥♥♡
Things To See ♥♥♥♥♡
Natural Beauty ♥♥♥♡♡

Oxford University

Drive Time to Oxford
From London | 2 hours
From Manchester | 3 hours
From Newcastle | 5 hours
From Birmingham | 1.5 hours
From Cardiff | 2.5 hours

Train Duration to Oxford
From London | 1 hour
From Manchester | 3 hours
From Newcastle | 4.5 hours
From Birmingham | 1 hour
From Cardiff | 2 hours

Best Time to Visit...
Summer - Tourism numbers are high all year round in Oxford but the summer months can be a little quieter as university students are on holiday. It's also a great time to enjoy river punting.
Winter - Visit in November and December to enjoy Oxford's wonderful Christmas markets and magical festive lights. Expect crowds, however!

Best Places to Eat & Drink...

The Spires Café | A cosy café in the heart of the city
99 Gloucester Green The Chilterns, Oxford OX1 2DF

The Olive Branch Café & Restaurant | Modern Mediterranean
17 Park End Street, Oxford OX1 1HR

Sartorelli's Pizza | Authentic wood-fired pizzas cooked in front of you
The Covered Market, 8 Market Street, Oxford OX1 3EF

No.1 Ship Street | A hidden restaurant with a romantic atmosphere
1 Ship Street, Oxford OX1 3DA

Arbequina | Independent Spanish tapas restaurant & bar
72-74 Cowley Rd, Oxford OX4 1JB

Top Tip: Bookworms should visit Blackwell Books, opened in 1879, the historic shop holds a Guinness Record for the largest bookselling room in the world.

Oxford City

Accommodation

£

Premier Inn Oxford Botley | 0333 015 0097
West Way, Botley, Oxford OX2 0JF

easyHotel Oxford | 0186 563 4602
280 Banbury Road, Oxford OX2 7DY

Travelodge Oxford Peartree Hotel | 0871 984 6206
Moto Service Area, Woodstock Rd, Oxford OX2 8JZ

££

Mercure Oxford Eastgate Hotel | 0186 524 8332
73 High Street, Oxford OX1 4BE

Royal Oxford Hotel | 0186 524 8432
Park End Street, Oxford OX1 1HR

Ethos Hotel Oxford | 0186 595 1740
59 Western Road Grandpont, Oxford OX1 4LF

£££

Old Parsonage Hotel | 0186 563 8170
1-3 Banbury Road, Oxford OX2 6NN

The Randolph Hotel by Graduate | 0344 879 9132
Beaumont St, Oxford OX1 2LN

Malmaison Oxford Castle | 0186 568 9944
3 Oxford Castle New Road, Oxford OX1 1AY

A Weekend Itinerary...

Day	Morning	Afternoon	Evening
Friday	Arrive in Oxford	Punting on the River Cherwell	Dinner at No.1 Ship Street
Saturday	Oxford University Tour	Lunch at the Olive Branch Café & Restaurant	Concert at the Sheldonian Theatre
Sunday	Visit the Covered Market	Explore the Ashmolean Museum	Travel home

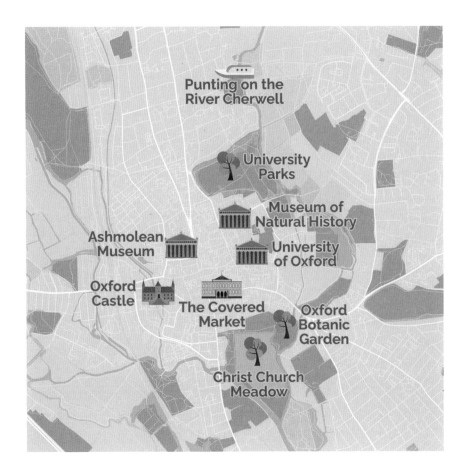

Punting on the
River Cherwell

University
Parks

Museum of
Natural History

Ashmolean
Museum

University
of Oxford

Oxford
Castle

The Covered
Market

Oxford
Botanic
Garden

Christ Church
Meadow

Best way to explore Oxford...

Most of Oxford City's attractions are all within walking distance, so you won't have to worry about catching taxis or trains once you arrive. There are, however, open top bus tours available to hop on and off.

 Did you know?

The University of Oxford is the oldest university in the English-speaking world, dating back to the 12th century. It also has ties to Hollywood, with many locations within the university being used as sets for the Harry Potter films, including the Bodleian Library and Christ Church College.

191

Top picks for slowing down...

Sheldonian Theatre
Broad Street, OX1 3AZ

Catch a concert or an event at the historic Sheldonian Theatre. Designed in the 17th century by Sir Christopher Wren, today the theatre hosts university graduations, concerts and special events. Once you step foot into this Grade 1 listed building, you can't help but be struck by its beauty and history.

Unique things to see & do...

The Covered Market
Market Street, OX1 3DZ

Originally set up in 1774 to keep the 'riff-raff' traders away from Oxford's main market, the Covered Market is now home to over 50 independent shops, cafés and bars. Open seven days a week, it is a perfect spot for a rainy day. Why not set yourselves a budget and sneak off to buy each other a gift while exploring?

Oxford University Tours
Multiple locations

Oxford's equivalent of 'when in Rome' has to be taking a tour of its prestigious university buildings. There are many tours available covering different locations, with the Bodleian Libraries being the famous spots on most tours. Getting to see the inside of some colleges will depend on whether you visit during term time.

Oxford Botanic Garden
Rose Lane, OX1 4AZ

For nature lovers, the Oxford Botanic Garden is a must-visit. Standing as the oldest botanic garden in the UK, it holds over 5,000 plant species and was originally built for medicinal research all the way back in 1621. If you plan to explore the garden on the weekends or holidays, pre-booking is recommended.

Harry Potter Tour of Oxford
5 Broad Street, OX1 3AJ

For all you wizards and witches, grab your wand and house robes, it's time to go to Hogwarts! OK, well not exactly, but touring the locations that inspired Harry Potter sets is the next best thing. Unfortunately, due to a *'no talking policy'* tours don't include a visit to Christchurch College, the inspiration for Hogwarts' Great Hall.

River Cherwell

Oxford Botanic Gardens

High Street

Oxford University

Top picks for adventure seekers...

Punting on the River Cherwell
Bardwell Road, OX2 6ST

What could be more romantic than punting down the peaceful River Cherwell together? It does take a little getting used to *(don't worry if you do fall in, you won't be the first or the last!)*. Don't fancy giving it a go? Book a chauffeured punt. Please note, most punt hire companies close from November to February.

Oxford Hot Air Balloon Ride
Oxford Ice Rink, Oxpens Road, OX1 1RX

Take to the skies with your loved one and see Oxford in all its scenic glory. Enjoy the stunning landscapes, from the historic University of Oxford buildings to the winding countryside surrounding the city. Rides are available March through October and you'll definitely need to pre-book for this one!

Budget-friendly finds...

Ashmolean Museum
Beaumont Street, OX1 2PH

The oldest public museum in Britain *(we told you there's lots of history in Oxford!)*, the Ashmolean Museum is home to collections that span cultures and continents. After a few hours of exploring and learning together, why not head up to the rooftop bar and restaurant for a drink and meal overlooking the city?

Modern Art Oxford
30 Pembroke Street, OX1 1BP

If you and your significant other enjoy the world of art, then this is the perfect budget-friendly afternoon out. Considered one of the UK's leading contemporary art galleries, it attracts some of the biggest names in modern art for its exhibitions. See if any workshops are on before visiting for a fun, bonding experience!

Our visit to Oxford...

We visited...

☐ Sheldonian Theatre

☐ Oxford Hot Air
Balloon Ride

☐ Oxford University Tour

☐ Ashmolean Museum

☐ Modern Art Oxford

☐ ....

☐ ....

☐ The Covered Market

☐ Punting on the
River Cherwell

☐ Harry Potter Tour

☐ Oxford Botanic Gardens

☐ ....

☐ ....

☐ ....

Notes...

....

....

....

....

....

....

Rating: ♡♡♡♡♡

194

*Our favourite photo
from the weekend*

Date:

Location:

Caption:

Winchester

A city rich in history, Winchester is well-known for its heritage. The district, which covers around 250 square miles, makes the ideal weekend away for couples who enjoy a mix of sightseeing and relaxation by taking advantage of the local independent restaurants, cafés and bars. Winchester is also the gateway to the South Downs National Park, making the city a perfect escape for couples who would like to put on their hiking boots while they're away.

Winchester City Museum

Romance ♥♥♥♥♡
Food & Drink ♥♥♥♡♡
Things To See ♥♥♥♡♡
Natural Beauty ♥♥♥♡♡

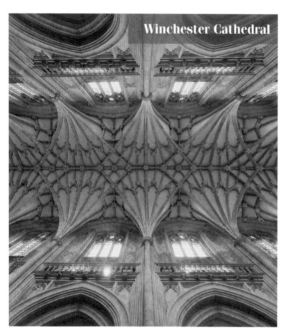

Winchester Cathedral

Drive Time to Winchester
From London | 1.5 hours
From Manchester | 4 hours
From Newcastle | 6 hours
From Birmingham | 2.5 hours
From Cardiff | 2.5 hours

Train Duration to Winchester
From London | 1 hour
From Manchester | 4 hours
From Newcastle | 5 hours
From Birmingham | 2.5 hours
From Cardiff | 2 hours

Best Time to Visit...
Summer - Take advantage of balmy weather and sunshine for sightseeing and leisurely walks.
Winter - Winchester comes alive at Christmas time and there is lots to do and see. Head to the Cathedral for a stroll around the Christmas market or drive over to Alresford to marvel at their Steam Railway Illuminations.

Best Places to Eat & Drink...

Josie's | The perfect place for breakfast
28 Jewry Street, Winchester SO23 8RY

Reeve The Baker | Bakery ideal for a quick bite to eat
41 High Street, Winchester SO23 9BL

Palm Pan Asia | A handy spot for lunch with a tempting tapas menu
166-167 High Street, Winchester SO23 9BA

Rick Stein | Seafood restaurant in the heart of the city centre
7-8 High Street, Winchester SO23 9JX

Chesil Rectory | Michelin star restaurant
1 Chesil Street, Winchester SO23 0HU

Top Tip: Take the South Downs Rambler bus out of the city to explore the South Downs Way, running every Sunday from mid-July to mid-September.

South Downs Way

Accommodation

£

The Westgate | 0196 282 0222
2 Romsey Road, Winchester SO23 8TP

Winchester Royal Hotel | 0330 102 7242
21-22 St. Peter Street, Winchester SO23 8BS

The Running Horse B&B | 0196 288 0218
88 Main Road, Littleton, Winchester SO22 6QS

££

The Winchester Hotel & Spa | 0196 270 9988
Worthy Lane, Winchester SO23 7AB

St Johns Croft B&B | 0196 285 4122
St Johns Croft, Blue Ball Hill, Winchester SO23 0AF

Northbrook Arms | 0196 277 4499
Stratton Lane, East Stratton, Winchester SO21 3DU

£££

The Old Vine | 0196 285 4616
The Old Vine, 8 Great Minster Street, Winchester SO23 9HA

South Winchester Lodges | 0196 282 0490
The Green, South Winchester Golf Club, Romsey Road, SO22 5SW

Lainston House Hotel | 0196 277 6088
Woodman Lane, Sparsholt, Winchester SO21 2LT

A Weekend Itinerary...

Day	Morning	Afternoon	Evening
Friday	Arrive in Winchester	Visit Winchester Cathedral	Dinner and drinks at Chesil Rectory
Saturday	Explore Abbey Gardens	Cocktail masterclass at Bombay Sapphire Distillery	Catch a show at Theatre Royal Winchester
Sunday	Visit the City Space at The Arc	Explore Marwell Zoo	Travel home

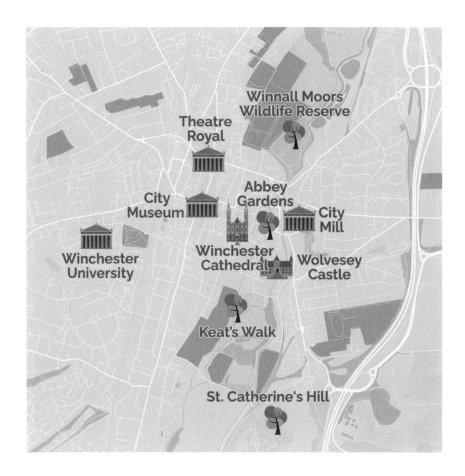

Best way to explore Winchester...

Most of Winchester's city centre attractions, shops and restaurants can be reached on foot. However, it may be handy to have a car if you'd like to venture a little further outside of town.

 Did you know?

Many popular films, TV series and documentaries have been filmed in Winchester and the surrounding areas. These include Netflix's The Crown, The Da Vinci Code, Les Misérables and Harry Potter!

Top picks for slowing down...

Theatre Royal Winchester
Jewry Street, SO23 8SB

A night at the theatre could be the perfect way to unwind after a busy day of exploring. Take your pick from the variety of musicals, tribute bands and comedians on offer throughout the year. Like most of Winchester, The Theatre Royal is also steeped in history and the building was previously a hotel and a cinema.

Abbey Gardens
65 The Broadway, SO23 9BE

Nestled in the heart of the city centre, Abbey Gardens and Abbey House offer a picturesque place to sit down and relax *(perhaps with an ice cream or picnic in the summer months!)* The gardens are a safe haven for nature and wildlife with the River Itchen running through the centre.

Unique things to see & do...

Bombay Sapphire Distillery
Laverstoke Mill, London Road, Whitchurch, RG28 7NR

This one is around 15 miles outside of the centre of Winchester; however, it's a must-see for gin lovers and those seeking a unique experience! Take a guided tour where you'll explore the glasshouses and botanical dry room *(all whilst enjoying a complimentary gin and tonic)* or book onto a cocktail masterclass.

Marwell Zoo
Colden Common, SO21 1JH

Museums not your thing? A short drive away from Winchester centre, Marwell Zoo sits on 140 acres and is home to a host of animals from giraffes to penguins and lemurs. It's also open 363 days a year *(closed on Christmas Day and Boxing Day)*, so you don't need to worry about visiting in season!

Winchester Christmas Market

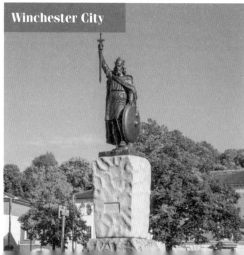
Winchester City

Winchester Cathedral

Top picks for culture seekers...

Winchester Cathedral
9 The Close, SO23 9LS

Take a guided tour around Winchester Cathedral and learn about the building's expansive history. Explore the Cathedral's crypt vaults, the Renaissance chapels, the grave of famous author Jane Austen and the Cathedral Tower for views across the city. Additional fees apply on top of the entry fee for guided tours.

City Space at The Arc
The Arc, Jewry Street, SO23 8SB

Art enthusiasts should pay a visit to the gallery space on the ground floor of The Arc in central Winchester to learn more about the city's thriving arts and heritage scene. The space hosts a variety of exhibitions, talks and activities throughout the year celebrating local artists and groups.

Winchester City Museum
The Square, SO23 9ES

If you're looking to learn more about the history of the city itself, Winchester City Museum is certainly the place to go. Take the journey from the city's Anglo-Saxon beginnings through a variety of artefacts, models and galleries. If you enjoy your time at the museum, you can visit again all year using your original ticket!

Budget-friendly finds...

St Catherine's Hill Nature Reserve
Garnier Road, SO23 9PA

Got your walking shoes with you? Climb 220ft up St Catherine's Hill and experience Winchester city centre and the Itchen Valley floodplains from a different angle. The reserve is bustling with wildlife and you might even spot some rare species of orchid dotted amongst the landscape in the summer months.

Our visit to Winchester...

We visited...

☐ Theatre Royal

☐ Marwell Zoo

☐ Winchester Cathedral

☐ City Space at The Arc

☐ ....

☐ ....

☐ ....

☐ Abbey Gardens

☐ Bombay Sapphire Distillery

☐ Winchester City Museum

☐ St Catherine's Hill Nature Reserve

☐ ....

☐ ....

☐ ....

Notes...

....

....

....

....

....

....

Rating: ♡♡♡♡♡

*Our favourite photo
from the weekend*

Date:

Location:

Caption:

Brighton

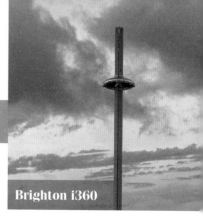
Best For: Independent bars and cafés, beach, pier, fairground rides & adventure.

A seaside destination with an inclusive, creative and colourful atmosphere – as well as its surroundings, where you'll find everything from buildings to beach huts coated in colour! Known as Britain's *(unofficial)* LGBTQIA+ capital, Brighton is packed with independent cafés, shops and bars all waiting to be explored. Head to the bustling seafront and enjoy the nostalgia of the palace pier, complete with arcades and fairground rides or sit back and relax together on a striped deck chair on the pebbled beach. Whatever floats your boat there's plenty to do here!

Romance ♥♥♥♥♡
Food & Drink ♥♥♥♥♥
Things To See ♥♥♥♡♡
Natural Beauty ♥♥♥♡♡

Drive Time to Brighton
From London | 2 hours
From Manchester | 5 hours
From Newcastle | 6 hours
From Birmingham | 3 hours
From Cardiff | 3.5 hours

Train Duration to Brighton
From London | 1 hour
From Manchester | 4 hours
From Newcastle | 5 hours
From Birmingham | 3.5 hours
From Cardiff | 4 hours

Brighton Palace Pier

Best Time to Visit...
As with all locations this seaside destination is best experienced in the sunshine, however, can be enjoyed at any time of year. Head to the Royal Pavilion Ice Rink over the winter season *(usually open Oct-Jan)*. Brighton Pride is held the first week of August if you want to join in on the festivities! *(or avoid if you're not keen on crowds)*.

Best Places to Eat & Drink...

Stoney Point | Great coffee and food
15 Montpelier Place, Brighton BN1 3BF

FIKA | Fried sandwiches, burgers & good coffee
Two locations; FIKA Beach @ Sealanes and FIKA Hove (Norton Road)

Halisco | Mexican small plates and tacos
64 Preston St, Brighton BN1 2HE

Wild Flor | Award-winning restaurant (lunch, dinner & private dining)
42 Church Road, Brighton BN3 2FN

The Little Fish Market | Tasting menu (one for a special treat!)
10 Upper Market St, Brighton BN3 1AS

Top Tip: Check out what seasonal events might be happening at the time of your visit at *visitbrighton.com/whats-on*. From comedy, to cabaret, to sporting events - there is usually alot going on!

Brighton Seafront

Accommodation

£

Hotel Nineteen | 0793 962 6831
19 Broad St, Kemptown, Brighton BN2 1TJ

Staybridge Suites Brighton | 0127 346 8805
1 Fleet St, Brighton BN1 4BF

One Broad Street | Book online
1 Broad St, Kemptown, Brighton BN2 1TJ

££

Harbour Hotel Brighton | 0127 332 3221
64 Kings Rd, Brighton BN1 1NA

Sea Spray Brighton | 0127 368 0332
25-26 New Steine, Kemptown, Brighton BN2 1PD

The Grand Brighton | 0127 322 4300
97-99 Kings Rd, Brighton BN1 2FW

£££

Drakes Hotel Brighton | 0127 369 6934
43-44 Marine Parade, Brighton BN2 1PE

Artist Residence Brighton | 0127 332 4302
33 Regency Square, Brighton BN1 2GG

The Twenty One | 0127 368 6450
21 Charlotte St, Kemptown, Brighton BN2 1AG

A Weekend Itinerary...

Day	Morning	Afternoon	Evening
Friday	Arrive in Brighton	Explore independent stores at The Lanes	Enjoy private dining at Wild Flor
Saturday	Enjoy the fairground rides on the Palace Pier	Indulge in a cake or two on the Brighton Regency Routemaster	Comedy or cabaret show at Ironworks Studio
Sunday	Head up the Brighton i360 or ride the Brighton zipline	Take a LGBTQIA+ History walking tour	Travel home

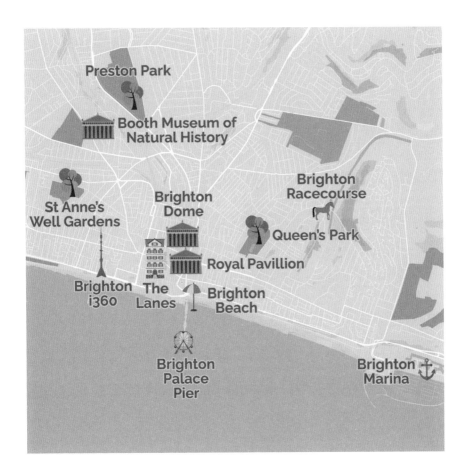

Best way to explore Brighton...

Brighton is compact and easily explorable on foot. Buses are plentiful and accessible for all if walking isn't possible. You could also rent a bike from one of the several rental spots along the seafront to explore a little further.

 Did you know?

Brighton is situated in the middle of a UNESCO World Biosphere Region. It also borders the picturesque South Downs National Park, which is an International Dark Sky Reserve.

Top picks for slowing down...

Brighton Regency Routemaster

Pool Valley Bus Station, BN1 1NJ

Relax and enjoy a traditional afternoon tea for two whilst aboard a restored Routemaster bus. You'll travel through the city from the Royal Pavilion to the Palace Pier, and along the seafront to the villages of Rottingdean and Saltdean. Pre-book online, where you'll find options to add prosecco or gin.

Unique things to see & do...

Brighton Palace Pier

Madeira Drive, BN2 1TW

Enjoy a fun filled afternoon on Brighton's 1,722ft long, Grade-II listed pleasure pier – home to an abundance of fairground rides, several restaurants, bars and arcades. Entry onto the pier itself is free, ride wristbands can be purchased online for a discounted price. Did you even go to Brighton if you didn't visit the pier?

LGBTQIA+ History Tour

Meeting point: Regency Square, BN1 2FG

Discover Britain's *(unofficial)* LGBTQIA+ capital with a 90-minute walking tour around Brighton. The *'Only in Brighton – Piers & Queers Walking Tour'* explores the history behind the destination of escape and freedom for those who didn't conform, from a lesbian, gay, bisexual, trans and queer perspective. Pre-book online.

Ironworks Studios

30 Cheapside, BN1 4GD

Fancy a night enjoying a comedy or cabaret show? Have a look at what's on at the inclusive and creative Ironworks Studios – home to one of Brighton's best comedy nights, *'Forge Comedy Club'* and cabaret, burlesque and drag shows. Book tickets to your show of choice online.

Brighton Palace Pier

Devil's Dyke

Brighton Pride

Brighton Seafront

Top picks for adventure seekers...

Brighton i360
Lower King's Road, BN1 2LN

Enjoy 360-degree views across Brighton in this 138m high observation tower. Why not head up for a romantic sunset and enjoy a drink from the Sky Bar? They even offer proposal packages...If you're feeling super adventurous, book onto one of the 'Extreme 360' experiences & walk, climb or drop from the tower!

Brighton Zip
Daltons Bastian, Madeira Drive, BN2 1TB

Thrill seeking couples could try out the longest zip line on the south coast! Enjoy panoramic views of the seafront from the 30-metre tower, as you glide for 300-metres above the beach alongside each other. Book online to secure your spot *(although they do except walk-ups)*. Save a few quid on a dual rider ticket.

Budget-friendly finds...

The Lanes
BN1 1HB

Spend a few hours exploring the narrow streets that are nestled between the seafront and North Laine. Independent stores, cafés, restaurants and pubs are all housed Brighton's artiest district – some of which dates back to the late 16th century, when Brighton was a small fishing town called Brighthelmstone.

Devil's Dyke
Devil's Dyke Rd, Brighton BN1 8YJ

Fancy escaping the hustle and bustle of Brighton centre? Head five miles north to the nearby Devil's Dyke, an area of outstanding natural beauty on the South Downs. Take a peaceful hike through one the dry valley and its surrounding landscape and soak in the panoramic views.

Undercliff Path
Brighton Marina, BN2 5UU

Take a walk *(or cycle)* along the Undercliff Path that follows the shoreline from Brighton Marina to the village of Saltdean. The uninterrupted walkway is about 5km long and makes for a peaceful escape from the busy Brighton seafront. There are several bike rental spots along the seafront if you'd prefer to cycle.

Our visit to Brighton...

We visited...

☐ Brighton Palace Pier

☐ Ironworks Studios

☐ Brighton i360

☐ Brighton Zip

☐ The Lanes

☐ ....

☐ ....

☐ Brighton Regency Routemaster

☐ LGBTQIA+ History Tour

☐ Devil's Dyke

☐ Undercliff Path

☐ ....

☐ ....

☐ ....

Notes...

....

....

....

....

....

....

Rating: ♡ ♡ ♡ ♡ ♡

210

*Our favourite photo
from the weekend*

Date:

Location:

Caption:

South West

Cotswolds

Cirencester

Best For: Countryside, hiking, adventure & romance.

The Cotswolds is an ideal place for a romantic break away, with its idyllic setting, picturesque rolling countryside and quaint towns and villages. The Cotswolds covers 800 square miles *(running through 5 different counties)* so you could spend many a weekend here exploring; however, we've picked out some of the highlights that you may want to look at first. Did you know the Cotswolds is an Area of Outstanding Natural Beauty?

Romance ♥♥♥♥♡
Food & Drink ♥♥♥♡♡
Things To See ♥♥♥♥♡
Natural Beauty ♥♥♥♥♥

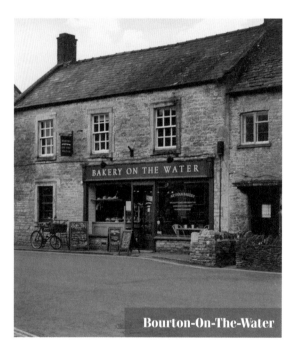

Bourton-On-The-Water

Drive Time to Cirencester
From London | 2 hours
From Manchester | 3 hours
From Newcastle | 5 hours
From Birmingham | 1.5 hours
From Cardiff | 2 hours

Train Duration to Cirencester
From London | 2 hours
From Manchester | 4 hours
From Newcastle | 5.3 hours
From Birmingham | 2 hours
From Cardiff | 2.5 hours

Best Time to Visit...
There's no bad time to visit the Cotswolds; in Spring there are fields of beautiful flowers and baby lambs. Summer offers the best chance of good weather for outdoor activities and the Autumn/Winter is the best time to enjoy cosy pubs and Christmas Markets.

Best Places to Eat & Drink...

Lynwood & Co | A cosy café for speciality coffee, cake & brunch
Several locations

Daylesford Café | Organic produce from breakfast to dinner
Daylesford Farm, near Kingham, Cotswolds GL56 0YG

Karibu | Exotic vegan bar and kitchen
No 23, Nelson St, Stroud GL5 2HH

The Pudding Club | Unique restaurant serving 7 traditional puddings
Three Ways House Hotel, Chapel Lane, Chipping Campden GL55 6SB

Sheep on Sheep Street | Eclectic restaurant & bar with amazing pizza's
Sheep St, Stow-on-the-Wold, Cheltenham GL54 1AU

Top Tip: The Cotswolds is a walkers paradise, so pack your walking boots and make use of the over 3,000 miles of public pathways weaving through it's scenic landscapes.

Broadway Tower & Park

Accommodation

£

The Bell & Stuart House | 0145 183 3669
Park St, Stow-on-the-Wold, Cheltenham GL54 1AJ

The Kings Arms | 0145 423 8245
The St, Didmarton, Badminton GL9 1DT

The Charlton Hotel | 0124 265 1051
London Rd, Charlton Kings, Cheltenham GL52 6UU

££

The Close Hotel | 0166 650 2272
Long St, Tetbury GL8 8AQ

Burford Lodge Hotel | 0199 382 3354
Oxford Rd, Burford OX18 4PH

Cherry Tree Glamping | 0771 772 1213
Seven Acres Rd, The Camp, Stroud GL6 7EU

£££

Feldon Valley | 0160 868 5633
Sutton Ln, Lower Brailes, Banbury OX15 5BB

The Manor House | 0124 978 2206
West St, Castle Combe, Chippenham SN14 7HX

Zen Den at Westley Farm | 0128 576 0262
Cowcombe Hill, Chalford, Stroud GL6 8HP

A Weekend Itinerary...

Day	Morning	Afternoon	Evening
Friday	Arrive in the Cotswolds	Explore Broadway Tower & Park	Dinner at Sheep on Sheep Street
Saturday	Wander around Bourton-on-the-Water	Get your adrenaline pumping at Cotswold Water Park	Go for dinner in Cirencester
Sunday	Take on a unique experience at Arctic Quest	Explore the Clearwell Caves	Travel home

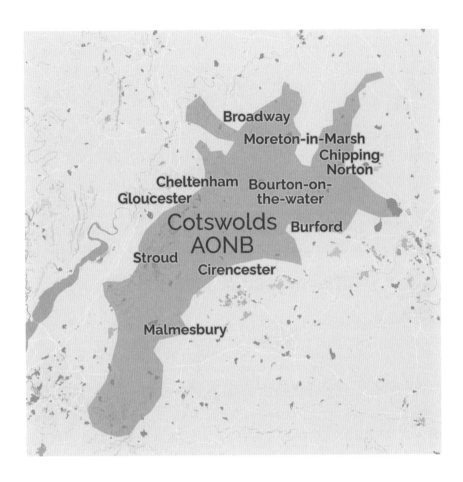

Best way to explore the Cotswolds...

Because the Cotswolds covers such a large area, its only really feasible by car. You can easily get the train from most large UK cities into Cirencester or Cheltenham and hire a car from there or use public transport to get around.

 Did you know?

The village of Bampton was used to film the village of 'Downton' in the TV series Downton Abbey. Are you fans of the show? You could take a guided walking tour around of all the filming locations.

Top picks for slowing down...

Bourton-On-The-Water
Cheltenham GL54 2BU

A quaint village on the River Windrush that's often referred to as *'Venice of the Cotswolds'* due to its stone footbridges. It can be very busy here so it's best to visit in the morning. There's plenty of shops, cafés and it's also home to the popular Cotswold Motoring Museum.

Dormy House Spa
Willersey Hill, Broadway WR12 7LF

Enjoy a range of indoor and outdoor facilities at this award-winning spa, including an infinity pool, thermal suite and *(for an additional fee)* the float tank - the perfect way to spend a romantic day together. Relax with a glass of fizz and bite to eat in The Greenhouse spa café. Various treatments are also available.

Unique things to see & do...

Arctic Quest
Croft Farm Water Park, Bredons Hardwick, Tewkesbury GL20 7EF

A truly unique and adrenaline filled activity for dog lovers! Learn how to control a team of huskies as they pull you along beautiful trails in the Cotswolds. After the activity, you can sit around the campfire, enjoy a hot drink and reminisce over your amazing "mushing experience". Pre-booking is essential for this one.

Cotswold Alpacas
The Dutch Barn, Cheltenham GL53 9NJ

Get up close and personal with alpacas! Opt for a 30-minute meet and greet or a longer walking experience. A wholesome way to spend a few hours, you'll take the alpacas on a scenic walk and then learn how to spin alpaca fleece into yarn. You could even book an 'exclusive experience for two'.

Broadway Tower & Park
Middle Hill, Broadway WR12 7LB

A perfect stop on your Cotswolds itinerary! Broadway Tower measures just over 1,000 ft making it the second-highest point in the Cotswolds. It's hardly a sky-scraper but it does make for beautiful views, especially from the viewing platform on the rooftop. Look out across the 200-acre's of surrounding parkland.

Chipping Campden

Cotswold Alpacas

Bourton-On-The-Water

Top picks for adventure seekers...

Clearwell Caves
The Rocks, Clearwell, Coleford
GL16 8JR

Explore this large natural cave system underneath the Royal Forest of Dean. You can opt for a standard entry ticket *(self-guided)*, a tour of the caves or, for the real adventurers, you can don a helmet, wellies and some overalls and venture even deeper – crawling and clambering down to 200ft underground!

Cotswold Water Park
Spring Lake, Station Rd, South
Cerney, Cirencester GL7 5TH

Fancy a challenge and some exhilaration? There are a range of activities on offer at Cotswold Water Park. Lakeside Ski & Wake are one of the top-rated companies here and offer water-skiing, wakeboarding and even inflatable rides! They also have a restaurant to chill out in after working up an appetite.

Budget-friendly finds...

The Thames Path
Beginning of the River Thames,
Cirencester GL7 6NZ

Stroll along the scenic pathway and soak up the quintessentially English countryside. The trail follows the River Thames from its source in the Cotswolds all the way into the centre of London *(for 185 miles!)*, so you'll only want to take on a small section. There's plenty of pretty villages for refreshment stops along the way.

Cirencester
Gloucestershire GL7 1BW

Considered to be the 'Capital of the Cotswolds', Cirencester is in fact its largest town. Yet another pretty town, this one is located on the River Churn and is bursting with shops, eateries, attractions and history! Explore the Roman Amphitheatre, play some mini golf at St Michael's Park or visit the bustling market square.

Our visit to the Cotswolds...

We visited...

☐ Bourton-On-The-Water   ☐ Dormy House Spa

☐ Arctic Quest   ☐ Cotswold Alpacas

☐ Clearwell Caves   ☐ Cotswold Water Park

☐ The Thames Path   ☐ Broadway Tower & Park

☐ Cirencester   ☐ ....

☐ ....   ☐ ....

☐ ....   ☐ ....

Notes...

....

....

....

....

....

....

Rating: ♡ ♡ ♡ ♡ ♡

*Our favourite photo
from the weekend*

Date:

Location:

Caption:

Bath

Pulteney Bridge

A beautiful, historic, thriving city, most famous for its ancient Roman Baths. The compact city centre is overflowing with places to eat, drink and shop as well as green spaces to enjoy, museums to visit and historical landmarks to discover. It's the ideal romantic destination for an enjoyable and relaxing weekend. Often seen as the jewel of the South West, Bath is regarded as one of the UK's best couples weekend getaways.

Bath City

Romance ♥♥♥♥♥
Food & Drink ♥♥♥♥♡
Things To See ♥♥♥♥♡
Natural Beauty ♥♥♥♥♡

Drive Time to Bath
From London | 3 hours
From Manchester | 4 hours
From Newcastle | 6 hours
From Birmingham | 2 hours
From Cardiff | 1.5 hours

Train Duration to Bath
From London | 2 hours
From Manchester | 4 hours
From Newcastle | 6 hours
From Birmingham | 2 hours
From Cardiff | 1.5 hours

Best Time to Visit...
Spring - Visit in March or April for a less crowded experience and potentially some decent weather.
Winter - Visit in November or December to enjoy the magical Bath Christmas Market, although it'll be super busy!

Best Places to Eat & Drink...

The Pump Room | Luxury afternoon tea & dining
Stall Street, Bath BA1 1LZ

The Oven | Wood-fired Neapolitan artisan pizza
3-4 Saw Close, Bath BA1 1EN

Green Park Brasserie | Independent live music restaurant
6 Green Park Station, Bath BA1 1JB

Sotto Sotto | Candlelit Italian restaurant
10 North Parade, Bath BA2 4AL

The Olive Tree | The only Michelin Star restaurant in Bath
4-7 Russell St, Bath BA1 2QF

Top Tip: Head to *visitbath.co.uk/special-offers* ahead of your trip to see what discounts and deals are available across attractions, eateries and transport.

Roman Baths

Accommodation

The Z Hotel Bath | 0122 561 3160
7 Saw Close, Bath BA1 1EY

Hampton By Hilton Bath City | 0122 596 7200
Avon Street, Bath BA1 1UP

Premier Inn Bath City Centre | 0333 321 9326
4 James Street West, Bath BA1 2BX

Abbey Hotel Bath | 0122 546 1603
North Parade, Bath BA1 1LF

Bath Boating Station Accommodation | Book Online
Forrester Road, Bath BA2 6QE

Apex City of Bath Hotel | 0122 541 8500
James Street West, Bath BA1 2DA

No.15 by GuestHouse | 0122 580 7015
15 Great Pulteney Street, Bath BA2 4B

Bathen House Boutique Hotel | 0122 580 5549
88 Newbridge Hill, Bath BA1 3QA

The Gainsborough Bath Spa | 0122 535 8888
Beau Street, Bath BA1 1QY

A Weekend Itinerary...

Day	Morning	Afternoon	Evening
Friday	Arrive in Bath	Explore Royal Victoria Park & the Jane Austen Centre	Thermae Bath Spa Twilight Session
Saturday	Visit Bath Abbey	Lunch at The Pump Room and Roman Baths Tour	Have a laugh at Komedia Bath, Krater Comedy Club
Sunday	Explore Pulteney Bridge	Enjoy a Bath Boating Experience	Travel home

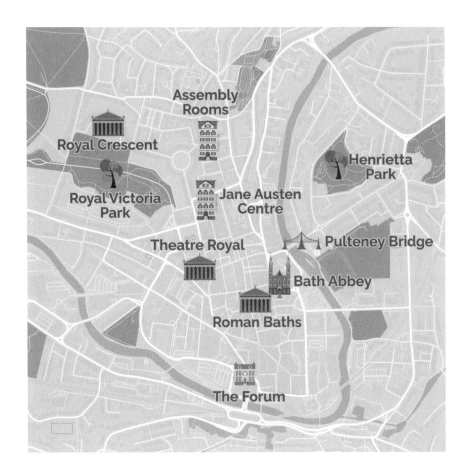

Best way to explore Bath...

The majority of Bath's attractions are within walking distance from each other, so Bath is best explored on foot. Alternatively, open top bus tours are also available to hop on and off as you please.

 Did you know?

Bath hosted the first UK farmer's market in 1997.
Today, there's a farmer's market held every Saturday mornings at Green Park Station. Visit and find fairly-priced, fresh seasonable products.

Top picks for slowing down...

Thermae Bath Spa
Hot Bath Street, BA1 1SJ

The ultimate way to relax and unwind within a romantic setting. The spa houses the only natural thermal hot springs in Britain and has a roof-top pool offering 360 views of the city *(a highly recommended experience we might add)*. Couples treatments are available. On a budget? Go for the Friday evening *'twilight'* session.

Komedia Bath
22 - 23 Westgate Street, BA1 1EP

Interested in a night of comedy? Head to Komedia, who host a 'Krater Comedy Club' event every Saturday night. This live entertainment venue is located inside a Grade II listed, restored cinema building and is home to a whole host of comedy, music, cabaret, club nights and more.

Unique things to see & do...

Roman Baths
Abbey Church Yard, BA1 1LZ

Visit what was once one of the finest religious spas of the ancient world. Today it's still filled with steaming spring water *(reaching 46°C)* and is one of the best-preserved Roman remains in the world. You'll take an audio tour around the museum and remains, why not combine with lunch at The Pump Room?

Bath Abbey
Abbey Churchyard, BA1 1LT

One of Bath's most recognisable landmarks! The impressive architecture of Bath Abbey makes for a wonderful Instagram shot, even if just viewed from the outside. If you're looking for breath taking views across the city then definitely pay the additional fee for the Bell Tower Tour.

Jane Austen Centre
40 Gay Street, BA1 2NT

Learn the story of Bath's most famous resident and author, Jane Austen, at this unique and insightful museum. The centre is located in-between The Circus and Queen Square, two of Bath's most historic landmarks. Why not stay for afternoon tea at The Regency Tea Room afterwards?

Pasta Laboratory
The Richmond Arms, 7 Richmond Place, BA1 5PZ

Get your aprons at the ready and learn the art of making fresh pasta by booking onto an experience at the Pasta Laboratory. The class lasts for around two and a half hours. Is it a special occasion? Why not book a private pasta making class for two, with a bottle of prosecco on arrival *(although it's quite pricey!)*.

Bath City

Bath Abbey

Bath Overview

Top picks for adventure seekers...

Bath Hot Air Balloon Ride
Royal Victoria Park, BA1 2LZ

View Bath from above! This isn't one for those scared of heights and is obviously weather depending; however, if this is the sort of thing that floats your boat (or balloon) then it'll certainly be a memorable experience to share with the one you love! Pre-booking is a must for this one.

Bath Boating Station
Forrester Road, BA2 6QE

Take to the waters on a romantic boat ride! Choose a rowing, canoeing or punting boat and head along the peaceful River Avon (the stretch between Bath and Bathampton) for an hour or two of fun – you could even pack a picnic to enjoy onboard? Please note they are closed during the winter months.

Budget-friendly finds...

Pulteney Bridge
Bridge Street, BA2 4AT

This historic bridge spans the River Avon and is an impressive example of Georgian architecture. It's the perfect spot to soak in the views, take a selfie and meander around the shops that line the bridge along both sides. The view from Grand Parade (southwest of the bridge) is the best spot.

Royal Victoria Park
Marlborough Lane, BA1 2NQ

A stunning public park, just a short distance from the city centre that spans a whopping 57-acres. There's a lot to be enjoyed here all year round, take a stroll along the Great Dell Aerial Walkway, challenge each other on the 18-hole mini golf course, or (if you happen to visit during winter) take to the open-air ice rink.

227

Our visit to Bath...

We visited...

- ☐ Thermae Bath Spa
- ☐ Komedia Bath
- ☐ Roman Baths
- ☐ Bath Abbey
- ☐ Jane Austen Centre
- ☐ ....
- ☐ ....

- ☐ Bath Hot Air Balloon Ride
- ☐ Bath Boating Station
- ☐ Pulteney Bridge
- ☐ Royal Victoria Park
- ☐ Pasta Laboratory
- ☐ ....
- ☐ ....

Notes...

....

....

....

....

....

....

Rating: ♡♡♡♡♡

*Our favourite photo
from the weekend*

Date:

Location:

Caption:

Plymouth

A picturesque coastal city, Plymouth is famous for its maritime past, breath-taking natural beauty and cobbled street Barbican district. It might be small in size, but it's mighty in spirit and a lovely destination for a romantic week-end getaway. From digging into fresh seafood to sipping gin from England's oldest distillery, this South West gem is a must-visit for any couple looking to slow down and unwind.

The Barbican

Romance ♥♥♥♥♡
Food & Drink ♥♥♥♥♡
Things To See ♥♥♥♥♡
Natural Beauty ♥♥♥♥♡

Royal William Yard

Drive Time to Plymouth
From London | 5 hours
From Manchester | 5.5 hours
From Newcastle | 7.5 hours
From Birmingham | 4 hours
From Cardiff | 3 hours

Train Duration to Plymouth
From London | 3.5 hours
From Manchester | 5.5 hours
From Newcastle | 7.5 hours
From Birmingham | 3.5 hours
From Cardiff | 3.5 hours

Best Time to Visit...
Summer - If you both hope to enjoy the local beaches and take a dip *(and don't want to freeze!)* June to August is the best time to visit.
Autumn - Visit in September to early November to enjoy Plymouth's natural beauty during its autumn bloom and expect far fewer crowds!

Best Places to Eat & Drink...

Kawaffle | Yummy sweet and savoury waffles
Cornwall Street Stall 131 Plymouth Market, Plymouth PL1 1PS

Jolly Jacks | Waterfront Bar & Bistro for breakfast, lunch & dinner
Richmond Walk, Mayflower Marina, Plymouth PL1 4LS

Cosmic Kitchen | Family-run vegan bistro
Palace Street Sir John Hawkins Square, Plymouth PL1 2AY

HonkyTonk Wine Library | Arty wine bar with food
2 North East Quay Corner of Harbour Ave, Sutton Harbour, Plymouth PL4 0BN

Fletcher's Restaurant | Coveted Michelin-starred restaurant
Gill Akaster House, 27 Princess St, Plymouth PL1 2EX

Top Tip: Climb the 93 steps to the top of Smeaton's Tower Lighthouse (that stands 72 foot high) for incredible views over Plymouth. Please note it's closed throughout winter.

The Hoe

Accommodation

£

Invicta Hotel | 0175 266 4997
11/12 Osborne Pl, Lockyer St, Plymouth PL1 2PU

Moxy Plymouth | 0175 242 2237
14 Millbay Road, Plymouth PL1 3LH

The Imperial Plymouth | 0175 222 7311
Hoe Court, Lockyer St, Plymouth PL1 2QD

££

No. 1 Elliot Terrace Apartments | 0333 666 9996
1 Elliot Terrace, Plymouth PL1 2QL

The Duke of Cornwall Hotel | 0175 227 5850
Millbay Road, Plymouth PL1 3LG

The Drake Hotel | 0175 222 9730
2 Windsor Villas, Lockyer St, Plymouth PL1 2QD

£££

Fox on the Hoe | 0736 540 3924
4 Elliot Terrace, Plymouth PL1 2PL

Rooms by Bistrot Pierre | 0175 226 2318
Residence One Royal William Yard PL1 3RP

Drakes Wharf @ Royal William Yard | 0333 666 9996
10 Clarence Royal William Yard, Plymouth PL1 3PA

A Weekend Itinerary...

Day	Morning	Afternoon	Evening
Friday	Arrive in Plymouth	Explore The Barbican	Catch a show at the Theatre Royal Plymouth
Saturday	Breakfast at Kawaffle	Take a tour at the Plymouth Gin Distillery	Dinner at Cosmic Kitchen
Sunday	Catch the Mount Edgcumbe Ferry	Explore The Hoe / Hoe Park	Travel home

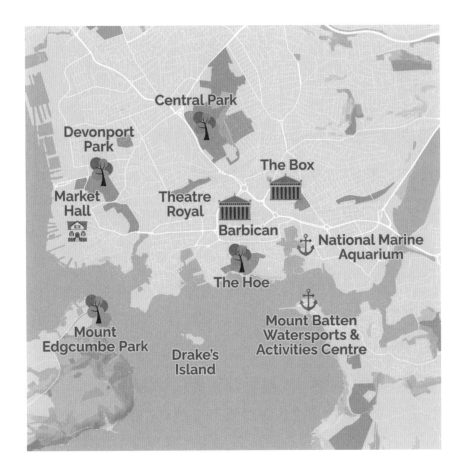

Best way to explore Plymouth...

Thanks to its small size and nearby attractions, most of Plymouth can easily be explored on foot. Local buses run to surrounding areas and ferries offer the opportunity to visit more difficult-to-reach spots.

 Did you know?

Plymouth has strong historical ties to the ocean and world exploration. It was the departure point for the Mayflower, the ship that carried the Pilgrims to the New World in 1620. It is also the birthplace of famous explorer, Sir Francis Drake.

Top picks for slowing down...

Theatre Royal Plymouth
Royal Parade, PL1 2TR

The UK's largest regional theatre, showcasing a wide range of musicals, classics and ballet. With new productions regularly arriving, be prepared to both be whisked away to magical theatrical worlds! Save some time to check out the work of local artists in 'the Gallery' on the first floor, too.

Unique things to see & do...

The Barbican
The Barbican, PL1 2LR

Plymouth's beautiful old port area, full of art galleries, cafés and independent shops, the Barbican is a delightful spot to spend an afternoon carelessly meandering its cobbled streets. Brimming with centuries of history, visit the Mayflower Steps or stand where Sir Francis Drake set sail on his voyage to South America.

Plymouth Gin Distillery
60 Southside Street,
The Barbican, PL1 2LQ

Take a tour of England's oldest working gin distillery right in the heart of Plymouth. Led by enthusiastic experts in the gin world, you and your partner will get the chance to learn about the history of the distillery as well as enjoy a tipple or two! There are three tours to choose from so make sure to book in advance.

National Marine Aquarium
Rope Walk, Coxside, PL4 0DX

Home to over 4,000 animals, the aquarium is the largest of its kind in the UK. Expect to come face-to-face with sharks, stingrays, jellyfish and two very cheeky turtles called Heidi and Friday! Peak and off-peak tickets both come with a complimentary Annual Pass for unlimited aquarium visits – yay!

The Market Hall
Duke Street, Devonport,
PL1 4PS

Blast off into space or dive deep below the ocean at Plymouth's 360° immersive dome. Once a thriving marketplace, the venue had a major revamp in 2013 and today it includes the 15m dome, a cosy café and co-working areas. Check out the website for the latest dome experiences and grab your tickets there!

Royal William Yard

...tional Marine Aquarium

Smeaton's Tower

Tinside Lido

Top picks for adventure seekers...

The Mount Edgcumbe Ferry
Barbican Landing Stage,
The Barbican, PL1 2NX

Hop aboard and feel the wind in your hair as you take to the water. You'll stop off at Royal William Yard, a hub for boutique shopping, and Cornwall's picturesque village of Cremyll. Time your return with the sunset for a moviesque romantic ending to the day! The service operates from late March to early November.

Mount Batten Watersports & Activities Centre
70 Lawrence Road, PL9 9SJ

An adventure playground and the perfect daytime date destination for unleashing your inner child! From sailing to paddleboarding to kayaking, you're guaranteed to have some fun on the water. Although open year-round (apart from the Christmas period), double-check the website before visiting for availability.

Budget-friendly finds...

The Box Plymouth
Tavistock Place, PL4 8AX

Have you ever wanted to see a woolly mammoth up close? Well, dream no more, introducing The Box and its life-sized woolly mammoth, Mildred (yes, she has a name!). One of the many incredible displays on offer at the museum & gallery, step back in time as you explore the fascinating history of England's South West!

The Hoe
Hoe Park, 4 Osborne Pl,
PL1 2PJ

Offering breath-taking panoramic views, Hoe Park is a natural harbour with expanses of green lawns. Enjoy a picnic here in the warmer months (or a dip in the nearby Tinside Lido) or a bracing walk in the winter. Make sure to visit Smeaton's Tower Lighthouse and Plymouth Sound (a stunning stretch of coastal landscape).

Our visit to Plymouth...

We visited...

☐ Theatre Royal Plymouth   ☐ The Barbican

☐ Plymouth Gin Distillery   ☐ The Market Hall

☐ The Mount   ☐ Mount Batten Watersports
  Edgcumbe Ferry   & Activities Centre

☐ National Marine Aquarium   ☐ The Box Plymouth

☐ The Hoe   ☐ ....

☐ ....   ☐ ....

☐ ....

Notes...

....

....

....

....

....

....

Rating: ♡♡♡♡♡

236

*Our favourite photo
from the weekend*

Date:

Location:

Caption:

Newquay

Lusty Glaze

A popular seaside town bordered by 7 miles of cliffs and glorious golden sandy beaches. Surfing has certainly put Newquay and the iconic Fistral Beach on the international map, creating a tourist spot with great nightspots, resorts, pubs, restaurants and a vibrant atmosphere! As well as the town centre and beaches, Newquay is home to attractions such as the Bluereef Aquarium and Newquay Zoo - generally there's a little something here for everyone!

Romance ♥♥♥♥♡
Food & Drink ♥♥♥♥♡
Things To See ♥♥♥♥♡
Natural Beauty ♥♥♥♥♡

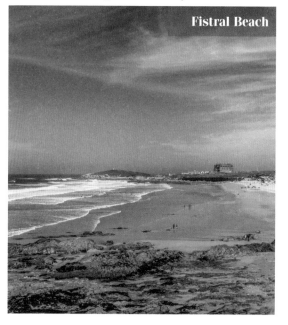
Fistral Beach

Drive Time to Newquay
From London | 5.5 hours
From Manchester | 6 hours
From Newcastle | 8 hours
From Birmingham | 4.5 hours
From Cardiff | 3.5 hours

Train Duration to Newquay
From London | 5.5 hours
From Manchester | 7.5 hours
From Newcastle | 9 hours
From Birmingham | 6 hours
From Cardiff | 6 hours

Best Time to Visit...
Spring – Hopefully you'll get some good weather and it's a quieter time to visit.
Summer – You'll get the best of the UK weather; however, it will be super busy *(especially during August when the Boardmasters Festival is on)*.
Winter - A quieter time to visit, however some attractions and eateries are closed for the winter months.

Best Places to Eat & Drink...

Gwenna Teahouse | Newquay's must visit tearoom
Beach Road, Porth, Newquay TR7 3LN

The Boathouse | Street food at Newquay Harbour
South Quay Hill, The Harbour, Newquay TR7 1HT

Lost Brewing Co | Café by day, bar by night - highly rated!
58 East Street, Newquay TR7 1BE

Toast Newquay | Tapas & wine bar
12a Central Square, Newquay TR7 1EU

The Fish House | Michelin seafood restaurant with a view!
Fistral Beach, Headland Road, Newquay TR7 1HY

Top Tip: Newquay beaches offer some great rock-pooling spots that are teeming with sea-life, so pack your bucket and net. Remember, if you move rocks please make sure you replace them.

Newquay Harbour

Accommodation

£

Great Western Hotel | 0163 787 2010
Cliff Road Narrowcliff, Newquay TR7 2NE

Travelodge Newquay Seafront | 0871 984 6244
Cliff Road, Newquay TR7 2NE

Premier Inn Newquay Seafront | 0330 128 1343
Narrowcliff, Newquay TR7 2PR

££

The Esplanade Hotel | 0163 787 3333
Esplanade, Newquay TR7 1PS

Lewinnick Lodge | 0163 787 8117
Pentire Headland, Newquay TR7 1QD

Porth Sands Beachfront Apartments | 0163 787 3274
Porth Beach Road, Porth TR7 3DR

£££

Watergate Bay Hotel | 0163 786 0543
On the beach, Watergate Bay TR8 4AA

Fistral Beach Hotel and Spa | 0163 785 2221
Fistral Beach, Newquay TR7 1PT

The Headland Hotel | 0163 787 2211
Fistral Beach, Headland Road, Newquay TR7 1EW

A Weekend Itinerary...

Day	Morning	Afternoon	Evening
Friday	Arrive in Newquay	Take a stroll along Porth Beach & Island	Tasty tapas at Toast Newquay
Saturday	Take on the waves at Fistral Beach	Discover the Bluereef Aquarium	Enjoy some seafood at The Fish House
Sunday	Head on a Newquay Sea Safari	Stroll along the South West Coast Path	Travel home

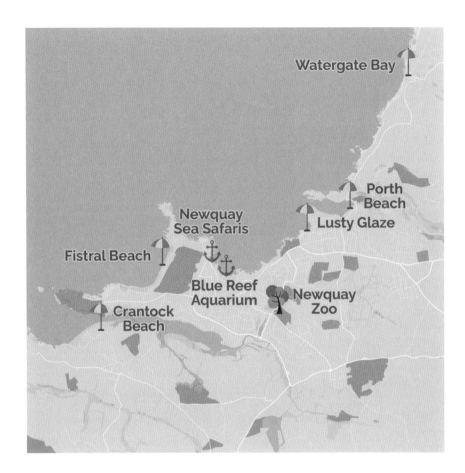

Best way to explore Newquay...

Newquay is easily explored on foot as its fairly small and compact. For example the zoo is about a 30 minute walk from the harbour. You could, if you'd prefer, rent an electric bike from Cornish Wave for a quicker way to get around.

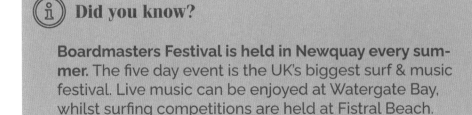

(i) **Did you know?**

Boardmasters Festival is held in Newquay every summer. The five day event is the UK's biggest surf & music festival. Live music can be enjoyed at Watergate Bay, whilst surfing competitions are held at Fistral Beach.

Top picks for slowing down...

Lusty Glaze
TR7 3AD

This magical beach offers a romantic escape. It somehow feels cut off from the rest of the world and is best enjoyed at sunset. There's a bar and restaurant *(that often hosts free live music evenings)* and an activity centre offering water sports. Access to the beach is via steep stairs but it's worth the climb!

Newquay Sea Safaris
Newquay Harbour, Sharks Head Kiosk 1, South Quay, TR7 1HR

Take a boat trip from Newquay Harbour out along and beyond the Cornish coastline, passing through Seal Cove – catch a glimpse of the grey seals that often follow the boat. If you're lucky you might even spot dolphins or basking sharks! Have a back-up if the weather isn't great as the trip might not go ahead.

Unique things to see & do...

Newquay Zoo
Trenance Gardens, TR7 2LZ

Are you both animal lovers? Spend the day at Newquay's 13-acre Zoo and visit the approx. 130 species there. Highlights include Lemur Island, the Penguin Pool and the Lion enclosure. Is it a special occasion? You could book an animal experience for an up-close interaction. Pre-book tickets online.

Bluereef Aquarium
Towan Promenade, TR7 1DU

An ideal activity for a rainy afternoon and those wanting to see an array of marine life including sharks, octopus, turtles and giant crabs *(to name a few!)*. Learn more about the creatures that live in our seas and oceans at one of the 'talk & feed' sessions. Pre-book tickets online.

Fistral Beach

Bluereef Aquarium

Watergate Bay

Newquay Zoo

Top picks for adventure seekers...

Surfing at Fistral Beach
TR7 1HY

Fistral Beach is a surfer's paradise! The sandy beach hosts many surf competitions and the popular Boardmasters Festival. As well as surf lessons and equipment hire, there are lots of facilities, cafés and shops located on the beach. Come on, you didn't go to Newquay without trying your hand at surfing did you?

Watersports at Watergate Bay
TR8 4AD

An ideal spot for adrenaline seeking couples (*on and off the water*), with surfing, kitesurfing, kayaking and paddleboarding hire and lessons on offer. There's also kite buggy and landboard rental for those wanting to stay dry. There's several beach side bars and cafés to enjoy here.

Pirates Quest Adventure Golf
St Michael's Road, TR7 1RA

Another rainy-day activity and some friendly, competitive fun with your loved one! A 12-hole adventure golf 'course' set inside interactive themed rooms, including the 'scare experience' (*don't worry you can take the 'safe passage' option if you'd prefer*). Pre-book online to secure your preferred timeslot.

Budget-friendly finds...

Porth Beach & Island
TR7 3LN

If you'd prefer a beach to relax or take a dip, Porth has spacious golden sands and safe bathing areas. Plus, surfing isn't permitted here during the summer (*although the waters are nice and flat and could be good for paddleboarding and kayaking*). Take a scenic stroll over to Porth Island, located next to the beach.

South West Coast Path
Lucky Elephant Rock, Newquay TR8 4AT

The South West Coast Path offers incredible coastal views across the entire region. You could walk all the way to the epic Bedruthan Steps (*sea stacks*), although this will take around 3 hours each way! Not feeling so energetic? Head to the 'Lucky Elephant Rock' which is around an hour each way.

Our visit to Newquay...

We visited...

☐ Lusty Glaze

☐ Newquay Sea Safaris

☐ Newquay Zoo

☐ Bluereef Aquarium

☐ Adventure Golf

☐ ....

☐ ....

☐ Fistral Beach

☐ Watergate Bay

☐ Porth Beach & Island

☐ South West Coast Path

☐ ....

☐ ....

☐ ....

Notes...

....

....

....

....

....

....

Rating: ♡♡♡♡♡

244

*Our favourite photo
from the weekend*

Date:

Location:

Caption:

St Ives

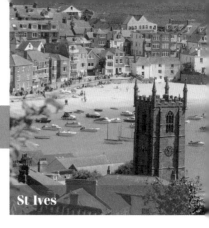
St Ives

This beautiful seaside town has an island-like setting with white sandy beaches galore and glimpses of the sea at every turn! St Ives is filled with picturesque cobbled streets, shops, eateries and a fishing harbour to explore. The Cornish town is famous for its links with art and is home to the Tate St Ives art gallery and the Barbara Hepworth Sculpture Gardens. The perfect getaway for beach loving couples!

Romance ♥♥♥♥♡
Food & Drink ♥♥♥♥♡
Things To See ♥♥♥♡♡
Natural Beauty ♥♥♥♥♡

Porthmeor Beach

Drive Time to St Ives
From London | 6 hours
From Manchester | 7 hours
From Newcastle | 8.5 hours
From Birmingham | 5.5 hours
From Cardiff | 4.5 hours

Train Duration to St Ives
From London | 5.5 hours
From Manchester | 7.5 hours
From Newcastle | 9 hours
From Birmingham | 6 hours
From Cardiff | 6 hours

Best Time to Visit...
Spring - Great for (hopefully) some good weather and less people.
Summer – Will be super busy; however, you'll get the best of the weather for days at the beach and water-based activities.
Winter - some attractions and eateries are closed for the winter months so be aware of this if you're planning to go for the quieter period.

246

Best Places to Eat & Drink...

Porthmeor Beach Café | Breakfast, lunch & tapas dining
Porthmeor Beach, St Ives TR26 1JZ

St Ives Bakery | Independent, delicious baked goods!
52 Fore Street, St Ives TR26 1HE

Harbour Fish & Chips | Traditional fish & chips
Wharf Road, Saint Ives TR26 1LF

One Fish Street | Highly rated fish & seafood
1 Fish Street, Saint Ives TR26 1LT

Cellar Bistro | Tasty dishes & romantic setting
29-31 Fore St, Saint Ives TR26 1HE

Top Tip: Pack your suncream (if visiting throughout the summer months), Cornwall possesses a mild and sunny climate due to the southerly latitude and the influence of the gulf stream.

Porthminster Beach

Accommodation

£

Tregenna Castle Resort | 0173 679 5254
Trelyon Avenue, St Ives TR26 2DE

St. Ives Bay Hotel | 0173 679 5106
The Terrace, Saint Ives TR26 2BP

Saltwater St Ives | 0739 108 6299
3 Belmont Terrace, Saint Ives TR26 1DZ

££

The White House at The Tinners Arms | 0173 679 6927
Zennor, Saint Ives TR26 3BY

Harbour Hotel St Ives | 0173 679 5221
The Terrace, St Ives TR26 2BN

Primrose House | 0173 679 4939
Primrose Valley, Saint Ives TR26 2ED

£££

Harbour View House | 0173 680 6130
Fernlea Terrace, St Ives, Cornwall TR26 2BH

Lifeboat Inn | 0173 679 4123
Wharf Road, Saint Ives TR26 1LF

Uno St Ives | 0742 833 8202
The Burrows, Saint Ives TR26 1GD

A Weekend Itinerary...

Day	Morning	Afternoon	Evening
Friday	Arrive in St Ives	Barbara Hepworth Museum & Sculpture Gardens / Tate St Ives	Enjoy some delicious seafood at One Fish Street
Saturday	Explore the Down-a-long Streets and Harbour	Enjoy a Sea Safari Boat Trip or Watersports Activity	Challenge yourselves at Escape Time
Sunday	Take a ride on the St Ives Railway	Explore Porthminster Beach	Travel home

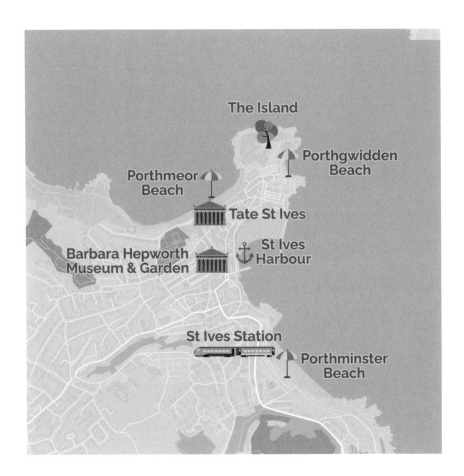

Best way to explore St Ives...

St Ives is small, compact and easily explored on foot. You could, if you'd prefer, rent an electric bike from St Ives ebikes for a quicker way to get around. Parking at the Trenwith car park and catching the bus into town is very convenient.

 Did you know?

St Ives is only 20 miles away from Lands End. The most westerly point of the whole of England. The landmark attraction is home to a range of experiences, a shopping village, restaurants and cafés, alongside scenic views and clifftop trails.

Top picks for slowing down...

Porthminster Beach
TR26 2EB

Relax or take a dip at the one of St Ives four beaches. It's surrounded by lush green hills and home to white sands, green-blue waters and palm trees – along with the mildest climate in the UK, it certainly has a tropical feel! There's a beach café, award-winning seafood restaurant and mini-18-hole golf course nearby.

St Ives Railway
St Ives Train Station, TR26 2GB

Want to experience one of the most scenic railway lines in Britain? Take the short *(10-15 minute)* 'Bay Line' train ride from St Ives to St Erth for epic coastal views, passing Hayle Towans and Carbis Bay. An off-peak return only costs around £4 per person and tickets can be purchased online.

Unique things to see & do...

Tate St Ives
Porthmeor Beach, TR26 1TG

Art loving couples should head to Tate St Ives, located behind Porthmeor Beach, overlooking the Atlantic Ocean. The gallery showcases changing international, modern and contemporary art exhibitions. Visit the rooftop café for spectacular views over the old town. We recommend pre-booking online.

Barbara Hepworth Museum & Sculpture Gardens
Barnoon Hill, TR26 1AD

Explore the life, work, studio and garden of the famous 20th-century sculptor Barbara Hepworth. A unique museum where her work is displayed permanently in the same place where she lived and worked from 1949 until 1975 *(a 10-minute walk from the Tate)*. Pre-booking online is recommended.

St Ives Harbour

St Ives Watersports

Tate St Ives

Sea Safari

Top picks for adventure seekers...

St Ives Watersports
Porthminster Beach, TR26 2EB

Feeling adventurous? You could both learn to surf, take a sea kayaking tour, hop on a paddleboard or enjoy a coasteering adventure with St Ives Surf School. Activities are located at Porthmeor and Porthminster beaches *(depending on your chosen activity)*. We recommend pre-booking online.

Sea Safari Boat Trip
Smeatons Pier, Wharf Road, TR26 1LP

Take a trip out to Seal Island *(as the name suggests, home to a colony of grey seals),* or Godrevy Island from the harbour. You could book the private boat hire option for a more intimate experience; however, its quite pricey! Pre-book online. Have a back-up if the weather isn't great as the trip might not go ahead.

Escape Time
Cornerstone House, Park Avenue, TR26 2DN

Try something different with this 60-minute escape room challenge. You'll need to work together *(and try to avoid any fallouts)* as you race against the clock to find clues and solve puzzles in order to escape! All bookings are private so even though it's the two of you, you won't be paired with others. Pre-book online.

Budget-friendly finds...

Down-a-long Streets
Fore Street, TR26 1HE

Take a wander through the old, lower part of St Ives that sits on a narrow ridge of land near the harbour. The cobbled streets are lined with whitewashed cottages, housing galleries, shops and eateries. Head to St Ives Bakery on Fore Street for a delicious, traditional Cornish pasty and sweet bakes!

St Ives to Portreath Coast Path
S W Coast Path, TR27 5ED

Enjoy walking and incredible scenery? Take a peaceful stroll along the South West Coast Path. The whole route could take around 6 hours each way, so enjoy as much or as little as you'd like. Godrevy Point and the North Cliffs are particularly beautiful, you could even drive to these points if you don't fancy the walk.

Our visit to St Ives...

We visited...

☐ Porthminster Beach

☐ St Ives Watersports

☐ St Ives to Portreath Coast Path

☐ St Ives Boat Trips

☐ Escape Time

☐ ....

☐ ....

☐ St Ives Railway

☐ Tate St Ives

☐ Barbara Hepworth Museum & Sculpture Gardens

☐ Down-a-long Streets

☐ ....

☐ ....

☐ ....

Notes...

....

....

....

....

....

....

Rating: ♡♡♡♡♡

*Our favourite photo
from the weekend*

Date:

Location:

Caption:

Northern Ireland

Causeway Coastal Route

Best For: Adventure, epic coastline, incredible scenery & natural beauty.

Fancy a mini road trip? Head for the Causeway Coastal Route in Northern Ireland, stretching from the city of Derry around the coast to Belfast. This signposted route takes in the very best of Northern Ireland and is ideal for a long weekend away. You can head in either direction, highlights on the route include the Giants Causeway, The Gobbins, Whiterocks Beach and Cranny Falls.

Cranny Falls

Romance ♥♥♥♡♡
Food & Drink ♥♥♡♡♡
Things To See ♥♥♥♥♥
Natural Beauty ♥♥♥♥♥

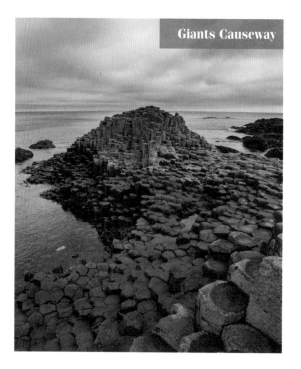
Giants Causeway

Drive Time to Derry
From Belfast | 1.5 hours
From Dublin | 3.5 hours

Ferry Time to Belfast
From Liverpool | 8 hours
From Cairnryan | 2 hours

Flight Duration to Belfast
From London | 1 hr 25 mins
From Manchester | 1 hr 5 mins
From Birmingham |1 hr 15 mins
From Edinburgh | 55 mins

Best Time to Visit...

Spring & Winter - Roads and points of interest will be quieter; accommodation availability will be good, and you might even get some deals. However, be prepared to deal with the cold weather!
Summer - Milder temperatures, longer days and less rain (although not guaranteed in Ireland).

Best Places to Eat & Drink...

Guapo | Fresh Mexican
69 Strand Road, Derry BT48 7AD

Igloo Pizza | Pizza truck
16 Eglinton Street, Portrush BT56 8DX

Bilberry Mill Café | Delicious breakfast & lunch
57A Main Street, Bushmills BT57 8QA

Maegden | Cheese toasties & dreamy hot chocolates!
119 Main Street, Bushmills BT57 8QB

Ursa Minor Bakehouse | Breads, sweet bakes & coffee
45 Ann Street, Ballycastle BT54 6AA

Top Tip: Consider becoming a National Trust Member to get free entry and parking at NT places across the UK & Ireland, such as the Giants Causeway and Carrick-a-Rede.

The Gobbins

Accommodation

£

Waterfoot Hotel | 0287 134 5500
Caw Roundabout, Clooney Rd, Derry BT47 6TB

Ballygally Castle Hotel | 0282 858 1066
Coast Rd, Ballygalley, Larne BT40 2QZ

The Fullerton Arms | 0282 076 9613
22 Main St, Ballintoy, Ballycastle BT54 6LX

££

Inn on the Coast | 0287 082 3509
50 Ballyreagh Rd, Portrush BT56 8LT

Shipquay Boutique Hotel | 0287 126 7266
15-17 Shipquay St, Derry BT48 6DJ

Bank Apartments | 0287 053 1476
60 Main St, Portrush BT56 8AN

£££

Marine Hotel Ballycastle | 0282 076 2222
1-3 North St, Ballycastle BT54 6BN

Aurora North Coast | 0776 194 5914
14 & 16 Castlenagree Rd, Bushmills BT57 8XN

Elephant Rock Hotel | 0287 087 8787
17 Lansdowne Cres, Portrush BT56 8AY

A Weekend Itinerary...

Day	Morning	Afternoon	Evening
Friday	Arrive in Derry	Explore Derry City	Dinner at Igloo Pizza
Saturday	Discover the incredible Giants Causeway	Brave the Carrick-a-Rede rope bridge	Grab a bite to eat in Bushmills
Sunday	Explore Kinbane Castle	Walk to Cranny Falls	Travel home

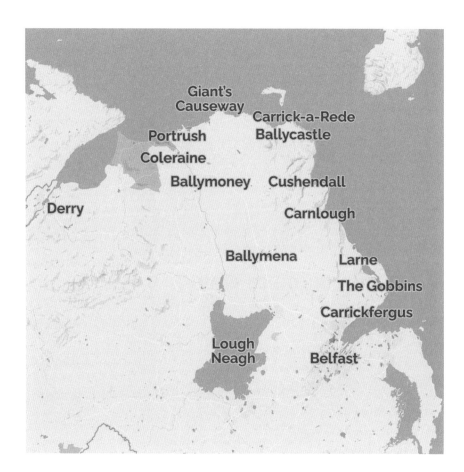

Best way to explore the Causeway Coast..

You'll need a car to travel from destination to destination along the Causeway Coastal Route. If you're travelling from Scotland, England or Wales you could hire a car *(or a campervan/motorhome to save on accommodation costs!)*. Alternatively, you could take your own vehicle over on the ferry. Ferries to Belfast are available from Liverpool and Cairnryan.

 Did you know?

Legend has it that the Giants Causeway was built by giant Fionn mac Cumhaill, a legendary warrior in Irish mythology. Science says that the basalt columns were formed by volcanic action 60 million years ago.

Top picks for slowing down...

Portstewart Strand
Portstewart BT55 7PG

Known locally as 'The Strand', this beach is one of Northern Ireland's finest and was used as a filming location in season 5 of Game of Thrones. The two-mile stretch of pristine sand is backed by 6,000 year old sand dunes which have been designated a Special Site of Scientific Interest. Park directly on the beach.

Whiterocks Beach
Portrush BT56 8NA

A beach with an incredible limestone cliff backdrop that really wouldn't look out of place in South East Asia! It gains regular blue flag status, has pristine turquoise waters and is a perfect spot for surfers and water sports fans – or a magical spot to just relax if you're lucky enough to get some sunshine.

Unique things to see & do...

Giants Causeway
Bushmills BT57 8SU

Visit Northern Ireland's UNESCO World Heritage Site and see over 40,000 of the iconic basalt columns that were formed over 60 million years ago. There is something unique and special about the Giants Causeways. Access is free; however, the Causeway Coast Car Park will cost £10 *(free for NT members)*.

Derry (Londonderry)
Derry BT48 7NN

The home of Ireland's only completely intact historic Walled City, Derry's vibrant city centre is filled with cosy pubs playing traditional music, a thriving food scene and a host of shops. The eye-opening Bogside history tour should be considered if you're looking to gain a better understanding of The Troubles.

Kinbane Castle
Ballycastle BT54 6LP

Breath-taking, in more ways than one! You'll need to walk down *(and back up)* the 140 steps to explore the castle itself – although, you can get fantastic views of the castle by walking halfway down the steps. The ruins of the castle sit on a graggy headland which looks mightily dramatic against the backdrop of the Atlantic.

Bushmills
Bushmills BT57 8SD

The gateway to Giant's Causeway! There's something charming about this village, with its quaint river side setting and cosy traditional Irish pubs. Whiskey making tours and tasting sessions at the world-famous Old Bushmills Distillery could be a fun and quirky activity to do together. Booking ahead online is advised.

Carrick-a-Rede

Whiterocks Beach

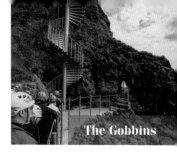
The Gobbins

Top picks for adventure seekers...

Carrick-a-Rede
Ballintoy BT54 6LS

Those with a fear of heights should avoid this one! You'll be walking across a rope bridge suspended some 100ft above the Atlantic Ocean. The scenery and coastline are stunning. If you are physically able, do the 2km walk from the car park. If you are GOT fans, add the nearby Larrybane Quarry to your list.

The Gobbins
66 Middle Road, Ballystrudder, Larne BT40 3SL

Branded as the 'Most Dramatic Coastal Walk in Europe', The Gobbins is a unique cliff walk experience with outstanding coastal scenery. You'll be walking across tubular bridges, climbing steps and exploring caves on this two-hour guided walk. If mobility is an issue, unfortunately this tour isn't for you.

Glenarrif Forest Park
Ballymena, BT44 0QX

Fancy a scenic walk? Head to one of the most under-rated locations on the Coastal Causeway Route! The park offers over 1,000 hectares of stunning woodland, lakes & waterfalls accessed through any of the 4 designated walking routes. The longest route (Scenic Trail) is 9km and the shortest *(Rainbow Trail)* is 0.9km.

Budget-friendly finds...

Cushendun Beach & Caves
4 Main Street, Cushendun, Ballymena BT44 0PH

Just a stone's throw from the village of Cushendun, the caves are another spot for GOT fans. They are believed to have formed over millions of years and can be easily explored in less than 10 minutes. From the harbour car park, cross the bridge over the river and immediately turn left to head back towards the sea.

Cranny Falls
Carnlough BT44 0LJ

One of the best waterfalls not only in Ireland, but the whole of the UK! The peaceful walk from the car park in Carnlough will take you around 25 minutes each way and is well paved. Once you reach the viewing platform, you'll be in awe of this magical 40ft waterfall which is surrounded by lush greenery.

Our visit to the Causeway Coast...

We visited...

☐ Portstewart Strand

☐ Whiterocks Beach

☐ Giants Causeway

☐ Kinbane Castle

☐ Bushmills

☐ ....

☐ ....

☐ Derry (Londonderry)

☐ Carrick-a-Rede

☐ The Gobbins

☐ Glenarrif Forest Park

☐ Cranny Falls

☐ ....

☐ ....

Notes...

....

....

....

....

....

....

Rating: ♡♡♡♡♡

*Our favourite photo
from the weekend*

Date:

Location:

Caption:

Belfast

Best For: Culture, history, good food, nightlife & award-winning museums.

Belfast is quickly emerging as one of Europe's top weekend break destinations. The city offers visitors a perfect mix of heritage, culture and damn right fun. Must-sees include the birthplace of RMS Titanic, the award-winning Titanic Belfast visitor attraction and the Black Cab Tour, which provides some powerful stories of Ireland's troubles. Belfast's thriving food, nightlife and art scene is centred in the Cathedral quarter, another place that must be explored.

Titanic Belfast

Romance ♥♥♥♡♡
Food & Drink ♥♥♥♥♥
Things To See ♥♥♥♥♡
Natural Beauty ♥♥♥♡♡

Cathedral Quarter

Drive Time to Belfast
From Derry | 1.5 hours
From Dublin | 2 hours

Ferry Time to Belfast
From Liverpool | 8 hours
From Cairnryan | 2 hours

Flight Duration to Belfast
From London | 1 hr 25 mins
From Manchester | 1 hr 5 mins
From Birmingham |1 hr 15 mins
From Edinburgh | 55 mins

Best Time to Visit...
Spring into Summer - The possibility of sunshine (although always a chance of rain in any season in Ireland!) and enjoying festivities such as St Patricks Day in March.
Winter - It might be cold but you'll get great deals on accommodation and there will be smaller crowds.

Best Places to Eat & Drink...

Bright's Restaurant | Traditional breakfasts & more
22-25 High Street, Belfast BT1 2AA

Panama Belfast | South American-inspired brunch
3 McClintock Street, Belfast BT2 7GL

John Long's | Fish and chips restaurant
39 Athol Street, Belfast BT12 4GX

Crown Liquor Saloon | The most famous pub in Belfast
46 Great Victoria Street, Belfast BT2 7BA

Coppi | Family-owned authentic Italian
Unit 2 St Anne's Square, Edward Street, Belfast BT1 2LR

Top Tip: If you take a tour of the Crumlin Road Jail you could head to the basement for a bite to eat afterwards. Cuffs Bar & Grill has a large menu, with several vegan and vegetarian options.

Belfast Castle & Cave Hill Country Park

Accommodation

£

The Gregory Guesthouse | 0289 099 5121
32 Eglantine Ave, Belfast BT9 6DX

Premier Inn Belfast City | 0333 777 3688
Alfred Street, Belfast BT2 8ED

Ibis Belfast City Centre | 0289 023 8888
100 Castle Street, Belfast BT1 1HF

££

Malmaison Belfast | 0289 600 1495
34-38 Victoria Street, BT1 3GH

Bullitt Hotel | 0289 590 0600
40a Church Ln, Belfast BT1 4QN

Hampton by Hilton Belfast City | 0870 590 9090
15 Hope Street, Belfast BT12 5EE

£££

Titanic Hotel Belfast | 0289 508 2000
Queens Road, Titanic Quarter, BT3 9DT

The Merchant Hotel | 028 9023 4888
16 Skipper Street, Belfast BT1 2DZ

Grand Central Hotel | 028 9023 1066
9-15 Bedford St, Belfast BT2 7FF

A Weekend Itinerary...

Day	Morning	Afternoon	Evening
Friday	Arrive in Belfast	Explore Belfast Castle & Cave Hill Country Park	Visit the most famous pub in Belfast, the Crown Liquor Saloon
Saturday	Explore Titanic Belfast	Wander around the Cathedral Quarter	Enjoy authentic Italian food at Coppi
Sunday	Take a tour around Crumlin Road Jail	Visit the Ulster Museum	Travel home

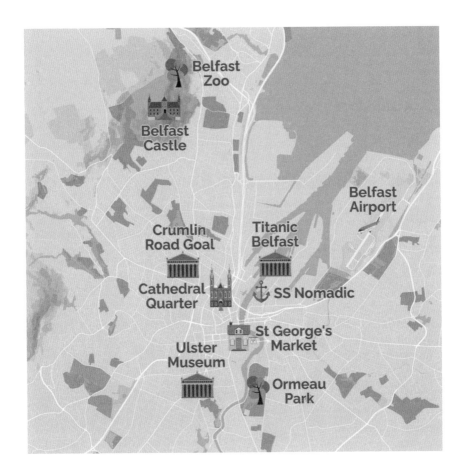

Best way to explore Belfast...

Belfast has a compact city centre and can be easily explored on foot. Bike rental is available if you'd prefer, and there are over 30 bike docking stations located across the city centre. You could also consider purchasing a 1 or 2 day ticket for the hop-on hop-off sightseeing bus which we always recommend for a more relaxing way to see the sights.

 Did you know?

Belfast has 3,000 acres of parks. From manicured gardens like Botanic Gardens to the forested Belvoir Park and Colin Glen, the city of Belfast has a huge variety of green space.

Top picks for slowing down...

The Merchant Spa
The Merchant Hotel,
16 Skipper Street, BT1 2DZ

Wanting somewhere to relax together? This hidden destination spa is located in the heart of Belfast city centre and welcomes non-hotel residents into its facilities. You can enjoy the relaxation room hydrotherapy area and a wide array of treatments. They will provide you with a robe, towel and slippers.

Unique things to see & do...

Belfast Zoo
Antrim Road, BT36 7PN

A great way to spend a couple of hours away from the hustle and bustle of the city centre. Belfast Zoo is home to over 1200 animals and more than 140 species, and set in a secluded part of Cavehill to the north of the city. The daily animal feed times are something to look out. Pre-book online.

Black Cab Tour
Book online – collection from anywhere in the city.

A famous Belfast Black Cab Tour is a unique and must do experience *(lasting around 90 minutes)* giving you an unbiased insight into the political murals and The Troubles. You'll visit important locations such as Falls and Shankill roads, the Peaceline *(Belfast's own Berlin Wall)* and many more.

Titanic Belfast
1 Olympic Way, BT3 9EP

Branded as a 'world-leading' attraction, this is a rite of passage for anyone visiting Belfast. The self-guided experience allows you to uncover the sights, sounds, smells and stories of the iconic ship, including an interactive ride and the chance to take your photo at the 'front' of the ship in true Jack and Rose style.

Titanic Quarter Belfast

Cave Hill

Belfast Castle

Top picks for adventure seekers...

Crumlin Road Jail
53-55 Crumlin Road, BT14 6ST

History lovers should head for a self-guided tour of Northern Ireland's only remaining Victorian era prison. Opened in 1846, the Gaol housed men women and children, before closing its doors in 1996. You'll explore different areas of the gaol including the tunnel, the hangman's cell, the graveyard and C-wing.

Belfast Castle & Cave Hill Country Park
Antrim Road, BT15 5GR

Explore the public rooms at the 1860s Belfast Castle *(one of the city's most iconic landmarks!)*. There's also a top-rated coffee shop on site. If you'd prefer a scenic walk, head along one of the three walking trails in Cave Hill Country Park – offering up incredible views over the city.

Budget-friendly finds...

Ulster Museum
Botanic Gardens, BT9 5AB

Great for history loving couples and those who appreciate art, from dinosaurs to mummys, archaeology to treasures...The museum is completely free to enter and offers a viable Belfast rainy day option. It is ideally located near to The Botanic Gardens *(another potential location to check out)*.

St George's Market
East Bridge Street, BT1 3NQ

The last standing Victorian covered market in Belfast! Your senses will come alive as your smell, touch, taste and see the vast range of fresh produce, delicious food and local arts and crafts. Known locally as Gorgeous St George's, the market has slightly different things to offer on each day it opens.

Cathedral Quarter
Donegall Street, BT1 2GQ

A trip to Belfast isn't complete without wandering the cobbled streets of the vibrant and buzzing Cathedral Quarter. The city's oldest and most beautiful buildings are filled with bars, restaurants and clubs. The Cathedral Quarter is home to some of Belfast's finest street art and is the cultural centre of the city.

Our visit to Belfast...

We visited...

☐ The Merchant Spa

☐ Belfast Zoo

☐ Black Cab Tour

☐ Titanic Belfast

☐ Crumlin Road Jail

☐ ....

☐ ....

☐ Belfast Castle & Cave Hill Country Park

☐ Ulster Museum

☐ St George's Market

☐ Cathedral Quarter

☐ ....

☐ ....

☐ ....

Notes...

....

....

....

....

....

....

Rating: ♡♡♡♡♡

*Our favourite photo
from the weekend*

Date:

Location:

Caption:

Index

Thank you...

We hope you've loved learning about these fabulous weekend getaways. Above all, our ultimate wish is that this book will help you create magical memories with your significant other.

We love a good quote and there's so many we could use here, but we'll leave you with this simple one ...

"Life is short and the world is wide. The sooner you start exploring it with the person you love, the better."
- Simon Raven

Editing & Composing – Robert Standley & Laura Mayes
Content – Robert Standley, Laura Mayes, Ella Mullett, Daniel John, Ben Skelton & Jess Goddard
Photography – Robert Standley
Additional Photography – Shutterstock, Adobe Stock & Unsplash

© Published by No Fuss Travel Guides | First Edition 2024
First published in Great Britain 2024
nofusstravelguides.com

Printed in the UK.